PHIL TAYLOR-GUCK

NO EXIT

LEVERAGING BUSINESS
PROFITS FOR LONG-TERM
WEALTH CREATION

R^ethink

First published in Great Britain in 2025
by Rethink Press (www.rethinkpress.com)

Contents

Introduction

Whenever I face one of those particularly tricky challenges that all business owners come up against now and again, I reflect upon a conversation that I had with a business coach some years back. At the time, I'd expressed my wish to offer my expertise to other businesspeople, capitalising on what I'd learned from many years at the helm of a number of companies. While I had done brilliantly up until that point (and, indeed, have done even better since), my motivation was to help others by sharing what I had learned and showing them how to avoid the mistakes that I had made along the way. Some of those mistakes had been extremely painful. Since I had experienced the lows, as well as the highs, of entrepreneurialism, wouldn't it be helpful to spread the word and shift the balance in favour of those successes? It seemed like the right thing to do.

'It'll never work,' the business coach said, shutting down the idea straight away, without a second thought. 'Failure is all part of the learning process.'

I didn't agree then and still don't today. Yes, we learn a lot from failure and we will all fail at some point, probably many times, especially if we are tackling something challenging. I am convinced, however, that now, more than ever before, we should all be helping each other as much as we can. Why waste time on mistakes that happen all the time and which are easily avoided? We can learn so much from what others get wrong. It is for this reason that I have ignored this coach completely and already written a series of books on the different aspects of being an entrepreneur, being candid about the good and the bad and the mistakes we all make. I've also shared my knowledge on every aspect of investing, another of my specialisms, to help those with an eye for growth make the most out of their wealth.

Dreams of a life-changing exit

In this, my latest book, I want to combine both areas of expertise to tackle something that is often on the mind of anyone who sets up a business: the exit. As an investor, I work with all types of high-performing businesses and have spent a lot of time in exploratory talks with businesses at various stages in their journey, many of which I don't subsequently invest in. As a result, I have had many conversations with founders about their hopes for the future.

Often, these conversations begin with stories about the past. Business owners will describe in detail their experiences of the first few years of setting up the company. As anyone in this position will know, this initial stage is often all about fighting to survive because this is the time when businesses are at their most vulnerable and when so many fail. There will be endless hours of work, juggling multiple roles and making sacrifices anyone who does not run a business will never understand. While there is excitement about building something from scratch, it is often overshadowed by the frustrations of slow progress, tight budgets and sleepless nights wondering if all the effort will pay off.

As time goes on, success will begin to feel closer, but the challenges will be greater. Hiring the best people becomes a gamble, scaling produces new complexities, and every step forward will seem to uncover new problems: problems that business owners could never have anticipated in their wildest dreams. Sure, they try to celebrate the small wins, but even these buoyant moments are fleeting. Friends and family may be encouraging about progress, but, even as they raise their glass, all a business owner can see are the issues that need fixing.

If the time comes when that business owner will cautiously admit that their company is moderately successful, the pride and pleasure will be overshadowed by the pressure. The business will demand more and more of them, leaving little room for a personal life. It's frustrating too, because it never seems to get any easier. Scaling and managing growth is just as challenging as it was in the early days. Meanwhile, new, more nimble competitors seem to spring up at an alarming rate, threatening to bring it all crashing down.

Yet, amid all the grind, year in and year out, there has been one thing that has kept them going, I am so often told. That thing is a bright beacon of hope in the future: the exit. These business owners are 100% certain that the day they sell their business will be the day they completely relax and just know it was all worth it. All that has gone before will be instantly forgotten.

Balancing your dreams with reality

Each time I hear about these ambitions for supposedly life-changing exits, I do my level best to steer business owners away from focussing on this goal. I do this for reasons aside from the reality that it is, in fact, rare for any business owner to walk away with those hoped-for millions, which is, let's face it, what you would need for an exit to be truly life changing. Those stories you read about serial entrepreneurs reaping extraordinary amounts for a few years' work are the exception rather than the rule. What concerns me, as an investor in multiple businesses, is that any strategy that fixates on the end result is hugely risky.

When businesses obsess over getting (and then perpetually keeping) themselves in good shape for a sale, they inevitably neglect the fundamentals. The longed-for exit becomes an unnecessary distraction just when they need to be on top of their game. This, in turn, manifests itself in a number of ways. Those making the decisions become cautious about investing in new products, or customer experiences, because they want the business to show a healthy annual profit to drive up the valuation. Meanwhile, far too much energy is spent chasing customers, any customers, even when their actual value on paper turns out to be dismal, thanks to the deep discounts made to acquire them. The basics – the strategies any business should be pursuing, which focus on the short and medium term and building revenue through a stable customer base – are forgotten.

I understand that the dream of a big payday is what many entrepreneurs rely upon for self-motivation. Believing that one day you will achieve that life-changing exit is enough to make you jump out of bed every morning and beam with pride (or grim determination) throughout the day, whatever challenges that day throws at you. The wise businessperson, however, wouldn't let themselves think about that – focussing their whole life on that single transaction.

Balancing your ambitions and aspirations with your current reality is one of the toughest and most important aspects to running a business and takes courage, strength, focus and objectivity. Of course it is much easier to keep your head in the clouds dreaming of an exit, believing you will make it, than to focus on the day-to-day. If you don't have a grip on reality and don't truly understand and analyse where you and your business are each day versus where you want to be, however, then you won't be able to make the right decisions. You won't be informed enough to take the actions you need to take and, importantly, you will miss out on the real opportunities.

Fixating on a single transaction is a waste of time and potentially damaging to the business, and almost always leads to disappointment. What these founders I speak to, indeed any founder, should be doing is learning how to build a successful, thriving and enduring business that generates those dreamed-of rewards from the start. Entrepreneurs should be thinking about how to enjoy the benefits of their efforts *every day*, in a regular and sustained way, not just on some far-off date in the future.

A new strategy for success

The strategy I am proposing in this book takes the focus 180 degrees away from the longed-for single transaction that will supposedly mark the pinnacle of a business owner's life's work. I have taken the whole idea of investing for the future more literally. Rather than expending blood, sweat and tears for a far-off, uncertain event, I propose starting to take some of the exit benefits *today*. The way to do this is to invest the surplus funds your business creates and get this cash working for you now so you can start living the life you crave straight away. Your hard-earned profits can generate healthy returns. There is zero point leaving it to pile up in a business bank account (with virtually zero interest) 'just in case'. Your profits can – and indeed should – become another important revenue stream.

For most business owners, this will require a completely different way of thinking about their income. It is not wrong to be risk-averse, especially with something as personal as a venture you have built from scratch. I am certainly not advocating gambling away your hard-earned revenue – far from it. What I am proposing here is a measured, well-considered strategy to make your profits work for you. This strategy won't be a distraction from the core business – it will enhance it. Additional funds generated by investments outside of the business can be used for growth and development. At a time when banks and other lenders are less than willing to play ball, this can be an essential lifeline when it comes to realising plans for expansion, whether by investing in R & D or bringing in new, highly talented, team members.

Prudent expansion will, of course, grow the revenue base. Just as importantly, business owners will be able to take some financial reward out of their companies today rather than wait for the exit. If you're goal-orientated, as most business founders are, this will go a long way towards solving the motivation issue. When you are properly remunerated, it helps you get through the more difficult times that all companies experience. The motivation derived from this ongoing approach, with tangible, regular rewards, far outweighs the motivation people get from dreams of a fruitful exit.

Achieving success with this strategy will require many of the entrepreneurial skills you already have. These are the skills that encouraged you to set up a business in the first place: ambition, determination, willingness to try things, being goal-driven and decisive and focussed on paying attention to detail. A bit of bloody-mindedness, where you don't want to follow the crowd fixating on a single transaction, wouldn't go amiss either.

It is normal for any business owner to work relentlessly towards success, and I will always encourage this, but we should work towards the *right* goals. Your purpose, passion and reason for being should not be consumed by dreams of an exit. Escape the single-transaction dilemma and make your business work for you. Every day.

Here's how.

ONE

The Single-Transaction Dilemma

he traditional view of the life cycle of a successful business owner is linear. In this rose-
tinted version, a highly talented and determined
person comes up with a world record-beating,
original idea, builds a fast-growing business on
the back of it, captures a healthy proportion of
the market and, when the going is good, heads
for the exit. Banks, private equity and venture
capitalists fight for the chance to give them
extraordinary sums of money. The business is
sold promptly to the highest bidder, with the
minimum of fuss, and then the talented founder

sails off into the sunset to enjoy a multimillion-aire's lifestyle.

Let's skip over the fact that this cliché is completely unrealistic. A truly original idea is rare. Most people build businesses around concepts that have existed forever; they just make their products or services a little better or are more accomplished salespeople. Building a business is tough too and the numbers of truly successful entrepreneurs are small. Most just about bump along OK, but many fail, often within the first few years.

The part I most want to talk about is the famed exit. The number of entrepreneurs who sell their businesses for a substantial sum is tiny. The amounts involved are certainly rarely life changing. In recent years, it has been even less likely that a business will sell at all. Here is the thing though: many business founders are *fixated* on the exit. They are completely convinced that all the blood, sweat and tears, the weekends worked, the big occasions missed will be worth it when the business sells. It will be a fitting culmination of a lifetime's work. Nothing else matters.

If you are that businessperson, and your retirement plans are reliant on selling your company, you are suffering from a bad case of single-transaction dilemma. This dilemma makes it impossible to see the obvious risks inherent in hinging everything on a plan to one day sell your business for a profit. What will happen if the sale doesn't deliver enough cash to realise the financial freedom you are counting upon? What if you don't manage to sell the company at all? What is plan B?

The motivations of potential business buyers are mostly the same: they want to buy a firm that is making money, will keep making money and, through their efforts at making it more efficient, will make even more money. It sounds like a simple list, right? Anyone with a profitable business might, at this point, be mentally rubbing their hands and thinking, *Let's get on with it*. Selling a business, however, is anything but a breeze, as the odds clearly show. The fact that a staggering 80% of businesses that go to market do not find a buyer speaks volumes. Indeed, if you are thinking about offloading a small business, or microbusiness,[1] that percentage of no-sales is over 95%.[2] The explanation for the latter figure is that the smaller the business, the more limited the options are in finding a buyer.

While selling a business feels like the ultimate financial milestone, the process is far more complicated than most owners imagine (with many failing to investigate this properly until just a few years before they sell, which can be an unpleasant surprise). What, then, gets in the way of a successful outcome for that 80% or even 95%? Traditionally, there have been just a small handful of reasons why businesses don't secure a buyer. We'll look at these in the remainder of this chapter.

Price

While some business owners will pluck a number out of the air when it comes to the price they'd like to sell their firm for, there's an obvious flaw to the plan. If the number is too high, no one will go near it. Too low, and a sale may have more chance of potentially just squeaking through but the business owner will be left out of pocket, wasting their years of hard work to build their company.

There are many businesses that specialise in organising these sales and they help companies navigate through the minefield of setting realistic price targets. They offer a bunch of different ways to make sure the valuation is a fair reflection of what a company is worth. One of the most common among these is a market-based approach, where a comparison is made with the deals achieved by other businesses which have recently sold in the sector or geographic location. The key here is finding firms that are of a similar size and revenue, have a comparable profitability and have sold in the recent past.

Most people selling their businesses will also bank their hopes on a hearty amount of goodwill. This revolves around persuading would-be buyers to think beyond the returns they can expect to make now and to also focus on what they may get in the future by trading the business more effectively.

If a buyer can be found, businesses should be able to, at the bare minimum, realise the value of the tangible assets, property, equipment, debtors and cash. This is most common with companies that rely on physical assets, such as manufacturers, construction businesses and retailers.

While there are a lot of different models for valuing a business, at the end of the day, the value of any business comes down to one thing: what the other party is prepared to pay for it. If no one is prepared to pay the asking price, or even negotiate, then the sale won't go through.

Market dynamics

The pace of change in business is fast. Super fast. It's accelerating too. Thanks to advances in AI and technology, many once rock-solid business sectors are no longer in demand. Industries which are widely expected to disappear altogether over the next ten years, or at least be radically changed, include delivery drivers, travel agencies, telemarketing and customer support, paralegal research, staffed retail stores and accountancy.[3]

Whatever business sector you are in, it is almost certain you have already considered the impact of technology and digitalisation on your future prospects. It stands to reason that a business with a short shelf life is unlikely to sell. Even if you are running a business in one of the most sought-after markets today, there are no guarantees that it will be part of the zeitgeist tomorrow or that a technology none of us has even yet imagined won't pop up and change everything. Up until 2007, most hotels and B & Bs felt quite secure that they were the only choice for people looking for holiday accommodation, and then along came a plucky little start-up called Airbnb. Disruptive businesses like Airbnb have popped up in sector after sector. There is a high chance, a *very* high chance, that if you haven't yet been impacted, you will.

It's not just digitalisation that represents a threat. A change in sentiment around a market can cause potentially catastrophic issues to a business seemingly overnight, particularly if it is mandated by the authorities. Think here of what would happen to some businesses if there were changes in environmental legislation. Any business perceived to be producing products that might be harmful to net-zero aims could find themselves in a difficult position. Not only would it become difficult to operate on a day-to-day basis, but no seller would even consider it as a prospect.

Timing

An exit dream is almost always linked to a specific timescale: *I will sell my business and retire before the age of sixty*. Occasionally too, a sale is forced upon us. Circumstances change, after all, and life can be unpredictable. Sometimes, businesses need to be sold rapidly because of unforeseen circumstances, such as a founder falling ill or a change in relationship between married founders. Unfortunately, the sales cycle isn't always accommodating to a strict timeline.

What happens if a business is going through a lean patch at the time it needs to sell? Perhaps it has recently lost a few good customers or seen its order book thinning out. Then there is the team. In a business of any size, there will always be individuals who are crucial to its success. What if a few of the most experienced and knowledgeable staff get wind of the forthcoming sale and decide it is time to move on to pastures new that offer more long-term stability? (It is the best people who always find it easy to find jobs elsewhere.) Each of these circumstances impacts the potential viability of a sale and will almost certainly reduce the valuation.

The time when you most want, or need, to sell will almost certainly not be the exact time a buyer wants to buy your business. If you simply have to follow through, they will sense your desperation and substantially knock down the price.

Economic cycle

Ah, you may be thinking, *I am not going to base this on my* personal *timing. I am going to build my sales process around the* economic *cycle.* The thinking here is that selling at the top of the market will ensure a healthy pool of eager buyers with deep pockets, which will make it easy to extract a premium price. Even then, there are risks. Selling a business is a protracted process, even when a buyer is lined up, ready to go. While negotiations might have begun at the market's peak, it never stays that way forever. That's basic economics. If the sale isn't completed swiftly, there is a danger that, when the market inevitably slows or inflation and interest rates rise, buyers will become more cautious and agreed deals will be devalued.

Even if the sale is somehow rushed through while everything still looks rosy, this doesn't always let the seller off the hook. Buyers are just as conscious of impending downturns and may insert a clause into the sales agreement deferring payment of at least part of the purchase price. Further payments will be spread over the following two to three years and might tie the seller into an agreement where the business must hit exceptionally ambitious future performance targets. Once the market does eventually hit its peak, however, the only way is down. Hitting these targets in a shrinking market is quite a challenge. Again, what this means is the big exit payday may not be as big after all.

Selling a business in a downturn can be equally onerous. Buyers are naturally more cautious about spending money in uncertain times. While in the thick of a recession, no one can be truly certain how long it will last, which makes it hard for buyers to commit. Even if a buyer is somehow secured, they may struggle to get the funding in place because lenders will be cautious too. Plus, when interest rates are high, everyone gets less bang for their buck, money-wise.

Trying to get the timing just right to coincide with the optimum economic conditions is difficult, even for the experts. Markets are notoriously volatile and things change rapidly. Businesses may be on the brink of signing a deal just as a downturn begins. Conversely, a strategy to wait it out until the economy looks less bleak may see businesses hanging on to their asset for far longer than they anticipated.

Increased risks today

If the odds of 80%, or even 95%, to agree a sale look bleak, I have bad news for you. Things are going to get a lot, lot worse. We are in the middle of a baby boomer retirement boom. Baby boomers are the generation that were born immediately after the Second World War, who have boosted the economy by working longer than many previous generations. This cohort is extremely entrepreneurial too, with large numbers leading the way in realising the dream of the free market by setting up and running their own businesses. According to one survey, more than 40% of UK small businesses have been started and are being run by this generation.[4] In the US, baby boomers own about 51% of privately held businesses, which are collectively valued at US$10 trillion.[5]

In what's been dubbed 'a silver tsunami of baby boomer retirements', 10,000 baby boomers are signing off work permanently every day in the US.[6] In the UK, over 11 million people, that's nearly 19% of the population, have hit retirement age.[7] For those among this number who followed their own entrepreneurial path, it is not unusual for their entire nest eggs to be tied up in the businesses they've built over their lifetimes. Baby boomer business owners need to sell because they're counting on the proceeds of their efforts for their retirement.

The natural laws of supply and demand are at play here. All the signs point to a substantial amount of baby boomer businesses hitting the market over the next few years. Indeed, there are already tens of thousands of businesses up for sale – even a cursory Google search will uncover a long list of options. This creates an unprecedented buyer's market, which will of course mean two things. Supply will (indeed, already does) outstrip demand, meaning only a certain number of businesses will ever sell. Of those that are fortunate enough to find a willing buyer, the increased competition will push prices down, so the benefit will be far lower than expected. Why pay top dollar for one business when you can just as easily buy another exactly like it for a lot less?

There's something else to consider here too. One of the strongest buying groups giving the boomer businesses the once-over are millennials, the generation born between 1981 and 1996. This cohort is squarely in the average age range of when people typically start a business.[8] On the plus side, they have cash to spend, having most likely already worked in the corporate world. There is a negative though. While this generation didn't grow up with a smartphone in their hand, they have been at the cusp of the technological revolution. Millennials have seen the power of digitalisation and how it has changed the world. They'll be looking for businesses that either already have strong potential in this sector or can easily be upgraded to take advantage of it. They are also acutely aware of issues concerning climate change. Sustainability will play a big role in the types of businesses they choose. Any businesses that are not seen to be in keeping with these ideals will struggle to attract a millennial buyer.

It's not just the boomer issue that needs to be reckoned with today. Business sellers need to weigh up the tax implications of a sale. Capital gains tax (CGT) is levied on the sale of assets, including businesses. In the UK, the higher rate of CGT was raised from 20% to 24% in the Autumn Budget 2024. While the CGT rate is still one of the lowest in Europe, behind France's 34% for high earners and Ireland's 33%, the change has been seen as off-putting for some sellers.

There have also been changes to Business Asset Disposal Relief, formerly known as Entrepreneurs' Relief. At the time of the Budget, business sales benefited from a reduced CGT rate of 10% on the first £1 million of gains. New rules will now see rates gradually increase, rising to 14% by April 2025, and it is expected that this will eventually align with the main lower CGT rate of 18% by the following year. For clarity, if a business was sold for £1 million before April 2025, there would be a saving of

£40,000 in CGT over selling it after that date. If it was sold after April 2026, there would be an additional £80,000 in taxes. It is quite likely that businesses planning to sell will have rushed to do so before the changes come into full effect, flooding the market still further. This will drive prices down and force sales in less-than-ideal conditions.

An increased tax liability will cut into the proceeds of a sale, which, if prices are already depressed, could be detrimental. The anticipated windfall could well end up being far less lucrative than expected, further complicating dreams of a comfortable retirement.

There's never a right time

It's a hackneyed phrase that 'there's never a right time to start a business'. The implication is that if you've got a good idea, you should take the plunge. Get started. Make it happen. Looking at the lengthy list of barriers to realising a successful exit, both traditional and more recent, I would go as far as to venture that it is

100% not a good time to sell a business. The odds of success, measured by creating a decent retirement pot, are vanishingly small and less enticing by the day.

Bear in mind also that it can take around five years of hard work to get a business sale-ready and maximise its valuation, which can be a huge distraction. For a start, the firm will almost certainly need to be completely reorganised and restructured so the business owner is leading it, not running it. Why? Because whoever buys the company will want to continue to trade it, so they need to feel confident that it can run brilliantly without the founder at the helm. There can be a need for additional investment to make these changes and ensure the business has all the resources to run independently.

Meanwhile, during this lengthy restructure, there is a job to be done to make sure all the best staff don't take fright and start polishing their CVs. Buyers will be looking to retain experienced, skilled workers who fully understand the business. It is possible to make sure key staff are tied in with options so they are unlikely to leave under new ownership, but, again, this requires more time and money. As if that is not enough to contend with, there is also work to be done improving margins so the balance sheet looks more attractive. This could be achieved by trimming costs, increasing productivity or raising prices a little. In addition, there is an argument for diversifying the offer so there is more to sell. Again, these actions risk spooking the troops and, at the same time, if customers are not impressed, it may impact sales – another important valuation metric.

Other presale actions include getting organised so the records are easy to navigate. Ditto, where appropriate, making sure all the relevant IP documentation is in place. After all, if you don't own the patent you've built your business around, there's nothing stopping someone simply copying it rather than paying a premium to acquire the company. Once more, though, these things take time and draw away attention from the core business.

Would any of the actions listed above be enough to transform the potential for a sale? Perhaps for a small number of firms, but for the most part I don't see them cutting through all the disadvantages that they bring with them.

There is, of course, an alternative to the challenging job of seeking a trade buyer. It might well be that you've got a talented top team who would be ideal to take over the reins. They know the business, they've worked with the clients and have good relationships with the suppliers and the employees. A management buyout (MBO) could be the solution to a smooth transition. It would also ensure the business stayed in the hands of experienced, committed individuals, which is important to business owners who inevitably have an emotional connection with the company they have founded.

While it sounds like the perfect solution, an MBO is not always the slam dunk result it appears to be at first glance. The senior team might not want to take over the business, with all the stress that goes with it. They may also not be at the stage in their lives where it is practical. They may have young children or commitments to care for an elderly relative.

It is quite possible they won't have the funds required to buy it, and getting external financing can be a hurdle. Banks might impose tough terms or expect a hefty deposit, while pitching to private equity funders is not everyone's cup of tea (or always successful).

What too if the management team don't agree with the business owner's valuation? They do, after all, know the business just as well and might want to drive a hard bargain. This could lead to a lengthy negotiation, with no guarantee that either side will be satisfied. In the worst-case scenario, the other side might even decide they are better off starting from scratch. They understand the sector and they can put their own imprint on it. This would leave the business owner in the worst possible situation. Their main exit option would be gone, as well as their experienced team.

An alternative strategy

All of this leads to the inevitable question: what happens if a business doesn't sell? Or, even if it does, generates only a fraction of the amount of cash the owner set their hopes on? The most obvious result is long-term financial insecurity. If the cash infusion was meant to fund a comfortable retirement, business owners will need to look for other sources of income. They might have to lower their expectations, dip into their savings or even continue running the business well into their old age. Some may decide to turn to family, inviting the next generation to take over. If this wasn't part of the succession plan, and is instead introduced as an urgent stopgap, it is inevitable it will put a strain on family relations. Family members might not want to run the business. They may also not be qualified to do so, which could negatively impact the business and the original owner's hope of salvaging at least something from the situation. The worst possible outcome is having to shutter the business without any gain having been realised. It is an outcome no one wants to even think about after years of hard work, but it happens more often than you would imagine.

I make no apology if this all sounds a bit gloomy – it is – but it is a realistic overview of the challenges any business owner will face if they are pinning their hopes on a lucrative exit. Focussing on a single transaction is not a viable plan for the vast majority of businesses. There has to be another way. The good news is that there is. Instead of building a strategy around that single goal of the Big Sale, the solution is corporate investing, where business owners build and retain wealth throughout the lifespan of a business. As well as reaping, and enjoying, the fruits of your labour sooner and on a more regular and sustained basis, there are far more certainties to this strategy. There are also plenty of chances to adjust and pivot if one strategy doesn't seem to be working. Plus, it can even help reduce your tax obligations year by year.

This solution will require discipline and patience, but not nearly as much patience as waiting it out for the lifetime of a business to cash in. Corporate investing will see you build greater wealth gradually and beat the single-transaction dilemma.

TWO

Creating Long-term Value By Investing Money From A Limited Company

A nyone who runs a business understands the importance of cash. As the saying goes, 'Businesses don't go bust, they run out of money.' This is a significant factor in why most businesses focus far too much of their energies on accumulating vast reserves, *just in case*...Strangely, though, many overshoot and end up with a huge pile of the stuff. While this might sound like a lovely problem to have, it isn't. Keeping a large amount of surplus cash stagnating in a bank account with zero, or minimal, interest doesn't do anyone any good. This money is not actively working for the business. It's not really doing anything. Not to mention the inherent risks to keeping large amounts of money in a single bank account. Customer deposits held by banks are protected by the Financial Services Compensation Scheme in the unlikely event the bank goes bust, but only up to £85,000.

Hoard cash by all means, but take steps to protect it and make it work for you and the business too.

The process that will allow you to do this is corporate investment. This is the term for when limited companies use any surplus earnings to invest in a range of opportunities instead of letting them stagnate in a bank account. Corporate investing is the practice of withdrawing money to place into carefully considered investments, giving a business the benefit of multiple revenue streams.

Corporate investing throughout the lifetime of a business is a more effective strategy to realise the value in that business than relying on the potentially elusive big sale. Why? Because it builds revenue incrementally and consistently. While there may be less income to invest at some times than at others, it's a strategy that will underpin a company's long-term financial health.

To properly understand the benefits, take as an example timing, one of the drawbacks we identified of relying on a single transaction. The year a business owner decides to sell, or needs to sell, might not be a good one, either for internal or external reasons. The business might be struggling against a more agile competitor, and thus not at its peak valuation, or the economy could be in downturn. Regular investments over an extended period iron out the shocks and make a business more resilient. If a sale is on the cards, it makes it possible to wait until a better time.

Something else identified as a potential barrier to a sale is shifts in the market. All businesses are vulnerable to disruptors in some shape or form, or changes in market sentiment.

Corporate investing offers an opportunity to spread revenue across a range of assets, all beyond the core operation of the company behind the investment. This reduces the risk of being tied to a single sector or income source. This is indispensable if a business is in a vulnerable industry, which these days everyone has to consider as a real possibility.

Creating value

The obvious question is: how do business owners personally benefit from regular corporate investing? In other words, how can this ever be something that is as exciting, fulfilling and lucrative as the big payday that comes with a sale? (Notwithstanding that this might not happen.) It is all well and good creating more money in the business on a day-to-day basis, but directors need to be able to access it. Taking it out via dividends has tax implications, particularly for those who already take the maximum amount available before being pushed up to the next tax bracket. While at least some excess profits can be assigned to tax-efficient vehicles like directors' pensions or top-ups to employee pensions, there is a limit on how much can be squirrelled away each year before it starts getting expensive.

Since we started with the exit, let's tackle that first. If a business owner is still intent on a sale, a company which owns a diversified portfolio of investments will be in a better position. Buyers are attracted to businesses that are less reliant on one core operation which is vulnerable to market forces.

Corporate investments even open up the possibility of a 'halfway house' option. A private equity firm might be persuaded to invest in, or acquire, a part of the business if the assets in question are perceived to be attractive enough in the medium to long term. In this scenario, the owner would still retain the main business but would have realised that sought-after payout.

In both scenarios, the investment strategy will have had an impact on the valuation. As the value of the investments grows, the balance sheet strengthens and the owner's stake will become worth more.

As we've seen, there is, of course, a high chance that a buyer can't be found. Again, though, the business owner who has consistently invested will still be better off. The option here is to close the business in the most tax-efficient way, pay the tax and pocket what's left. Corporate investing increases the amount of money held by a business. More cash in the business equals a bigger payout. It's that simple.

There are more immediate advantages too, which will improve the day-to-day business operation. Money makes money. Many banks will allow companies to take out loans secured against assets like stock portfolios. These 'margin loans' or 'secured loans' are a source of cash, without having to sell off the asset, and can be used to expand and grow the business. It might sound ambitious (and will turn the whole idea of the exit on its head), but there is nothing to stop businesses using this money to buy other, smaller businesses in complementary sectors.

Imagine a scenario where, say, an established electronics manufacturer invests in a number of electronics start-ups. Thanks to their experience and knowledge of the sector, the manufacturer will be in a good position to know which start-ups have real potential, certainly more so than buyers who are not steeped in the business. As well as having a good chance of backing a winner and generating high returns, this strategy will increase the parent company's reach and influence and create multiple revenue streams.

Once on the acquisition trail, businesses can think about buying firms on the basis that they offer a complementary skill which will help them expand and gradually diversify the core business. Another example here might be a niche clothing company selling cutting-edge garments to a small, but loyal, fanbase of fashionistas. Breaking it down, the business owner might see that the company's real competencies lie in its inventory management and fulfilment capabilities. This business sits atop a sophisticated ordering and stock control system that could improve the market for just about anything. It could just as easily be selling and delivering sofas or laser printers, instead of skirts and dresses. Thus, the business owner might think about buying a small home and kitchenware business, or indeed any other firm which requires a top-notch delivery system. Again, if the funds are available, this can be a great way of reinvesting profits while growing and strengthening the core business.

Even without a loan, businesses can invest the gains from corporate investment in a diverse range of ways, strengthening the business overall without incurring more tax. Traditionally, a company might borrow money from the bank to fund growth plans, or approach external investors for cash. The latter option always involves a significant decision because it entails giving away equity in the business. With an investment strategy, surplus cash can be used for growth and expansion projects which will, in turn, generate more income. No debt, or shares giveaway, is required. There will be additional tax relief benefits for certain sectors if the types of activities being funded are in the area of innovation or R & D. R & D tax relief allows companies working on innovative projects in science and technology to deduct an extra 86% of qualifying costs from trading profits, over and above the normal 100% deduction, to make a total of 186%.

Another smart investment tactic would be to use money to up the quality of the team. Employing more experienced executives, team leaders and managers will cost more in terms of salaries and bonuses, but they should more than pay that back with what they bring to the party and the improvements they make to the core business. This will further strengthen the firm's financial position, and the compensation is accounted for as a legitimate business expense.

Exponential growth versus one-off sale

When I started looking into investment strategies some years ago, I spent time investigating the Warren Buffett school of thinking. As he is one of the most successful investors in the world, and an inspiration for any investor, I figured he probably knew what to look out for.

When it comes to the key to his success, one investment strategy has been a game changer. He has built his strategy around the impact of time and compounding and it has underpinned everything he does. He eloquently describes this in his authorised biography, *The Snowball: Warren Buffett and the Business of Life*.[9] Life is, he says, like a snowball – 'The important thing is finding wet snow and a really long hill.' In other words, he reinvested what profit he made, which in turn led to an exponential growth in wealth – or snowball effect – when the stocks rose in value. This is the magic of compounding and time combined.

To understand the power of compounding, consider the classic question: 'What would you rather: £1 million today or to take a penny and see it double in value every day for the next thirty days?'

Many people instinctively plump for the £1 million. It's a big and tempting figure. If you know anything about compounding, though, you'll understand that by the end of thirty days, that once modest penny will have soared in value to be worth over £5 million. This, in a nutshell, describes the exponential power of compounding when small gains are reinvested. The time component is crucial here too. Initially, the results of compounding might seem insignificant: 1p becomes 2p, 2p becomes 4p. As the investment period lengthens, the compounding effect creates an aggressive growth curve. While that penny has grown only to £163.84 by day fifteen, it will have arrived at a respectable valuation of £167,772.16 just ten days later. By day twenty-eight, it will have sailed past the £1 million mark. If you were the person who took the £1 million cash, you'd be gutted on days twenty-nine and thirty, when the penny grew to £4 million. Start the process with more than that penny, and it is easy to see that the upside can be impressive.

Compounding is a crucial component in any corporate investment strategy and the polar opposite of waiting until retirement for the big payout. Here, business owners regularly drip-feed small amounts into investments and then leave the money to grow. Now think about the difference between the growth in compounding interest and regular interest. Regular interest growth is calculated on the initial, or principal, balance. With compounding interest, each year's interest is added to the initial balance, creating a new, larger balance. Thus, the reinvested sum starts to earn interest of its own, helping the initial balance to grow much faster. You are basically earning interest on your interest.

To give a real-world example of how powerful this can be, take an investment fund that tracks the FTSE 100 Index. The FTSE 100 Index closed at 4,476 points on 31 December 2003.[10] Twenty years later, on 29 December 2023, it closed at 7,733 points,[11] representing a rise of 72%. If you'd invested £10,000 at the beginning of the period and taken the dividends as an income, your investment would have been worth £17,270 at the end. That's not a bad result. If you had reinvested the dividends, however, your £10K would have almost tripled to £26,379. The difference between reinvesting and not reinvesting is almost equivalent to the initial £10,000 stake.

Depending upon the size of your initial investment, these returns can start to add up, especially over ten or twenty years or longer. The absolute rule here is: the longer you give it, the more you will make. One of the most successful investors of all time is James Simons, the head of the hedge fund Renaissance Technologies. Before he passed away in 2024 at eighty-six years old, he was able to compound money at 66% a year. The money-making success of the mathematician and codebreaker eclipsed that of even Buffett, who has compounded at a more modest (but still respectable) 22% annually.[12] The only reason Warren Buffett has been able to accumulate significantly more wealth is he got a head start. Mr Simons didn't start down this path until he was fifty, giving him less than half as many years at this strategy than Mr Buffett, who has been investing over a seventy-year time span. It has been calculated that if James Simons had earned this 66% return for the same length of time, he'd have been worth more than sixty-three *quintillion* dollars. If you want to think about it in figures, that is 63 followed by eighteen 0s.

Changing your mindset

There is, of course, an option to do nothing. After all, having spare cash in a business is not a negative. It gives peace of mind that there is something to fall back on when the unexpected happens. There is another way of looking at it too. Imagine you have a cash surplus of £40,000 sitting in your business bank account, after taking into account cash flow and all the bills due over the next year, including VAT and corporation tax. At the time of writing, according to Moneyfacts, the best interest rate available in an easy access savings account is 4.37%. Assuming interest is paid annually, your £40,000 will have increased to £41,748 in a year's time.[13]

Now, let's set that against inflation. The Office for National Statistics says the rate of inflation to August 2024 was 2.2%.[14] This means that £40,000 of goods and services would cost £40,880 after a year of inflation at 2.2%. While the surplus cash in your account grows in value to £41,748, it loses £868 in spending power while sitting in the bank. Keeping cash on hand is always a good strategy, but too much cash left lying around simply erodes in value. This is another key reason why investing surplus cash is a credible tactic.

Even though the figures tell a story, I can understand why you may still be reluctant. Long-term investing of any sort requires patience and discipline. Human psychology makes us more inclined to seek out immediate rewards and some sort of certainty over time. While business owners may be able to convince themselves to be patient for the eventual sale of the firm, largely because they still believe the payout will be significant, they may find it difficult to get used to the idea of 'tying money up' in investments and leaving it to grow. It doesn't help that the benefits of compounding are not dramatic at first. Indeed, they can seem insignificant, with any worthwhile potential gain deferred to a far-off date. Anyone used to running their own business will know how fast-paced it can be, with multiple decisions needed to be made on a daily basis. This might all seem a bit, well, slow. Besides, with gains that small, wouldn't they be better off investing only in the day-to-day operations of the business? After all, it stands to reason that the person in charge understands the core needs of a business best, far more so than putting money into external investments that may be out of their area of expertise.

This last point is pivotal to escaping single-transaction dilemma. Overconfidence in the core business and the prospects of a sale can result in a lack of diversification and leave owners overly dependent on their primary income stream. You need to change your mindset and remind yourself of the real benefits to forgetting about the one-off sale. The goal of creating a comfortable retirement and realising the maximum value of a business needs to be broken into smaller, achievable and, in the long term, more lucrative milestones. While the requirement for patience can be challenging, business owners need to commit to staying the course to give compounding time to work its magic.

How much, then, should you commit to your compounding fund? Since it is natural – and completely right – to have concerns about the core business and preserving the strength of the asset, it is wise to think carefully about the size of any investment. To be successful, compounding requires continual investment of returns. Any withdrawal of cash from the main investment fund, even temporarily, will slow the potential impact down and reduce the snowball effect. Not only is the capital lost but also the future income that capital would have earned through dividends. This loss can prove to be substantial in the long term, even if the amount taken is quite small.

As with any new strategy, the answer to the success of compounding lies in making a careful assessment of the current assets, clearly defining goals and creating, and then sticking to, a plan.

THREE

Getting Started: How Much Should You Invest And How?

When a business makes a profit, the owner has two options when it comes to what to do with that surplus cash. They could withdraw the money as dividends for their personal use, or they could retain the profits in the business, pay the relevant taxes and invest the remaining amount through corporate investments. The former approach has drawbacks, not least that it complicates the owner's tax situation because they will be taking money out as an individual.

Withdrawing money for anything other than core business expenses can be seen as paying an additional dividend, which means there will be income tax to pay. If the sum involved pushes the business into another tax bracket, it can be an expensive way to borrow.

Possible scenarios

To show why this puts you at a disadvantage, let's look at the figures behind both scenarios. Imagine you have calculated that there is £100,000 of surplus cash in the business at the end of the financial year.

Scenario one: Taking £100,000 as a dividend

In the UK, corporate profits are first subject to corporation tax before dividends can be distributed.

Current corporation tax rate: 25%

On £100,000 profit, corporation tax = £100,000 × 25% = £25,000

This leaves £75,000 available for dividends

Once dividends are paid, an individual will be taxed on the amount they take. The rate will vary according to their tax bracket, but let's assume this is a higher rate taxpayer.

Dividend tax allowance: £1,000 (tax free)

Taxable dividend =
£75,000 – £1,000 = £74,000

Higher rate dividend tax rate: 33.75%

Dividend tax liability =
£74,000 × 33.75% = £24,975

Therefore, in this scenario, the total taxes paid are:

Corporation tax: £25,000

Dividend tax: £24,975

Total: £49,975

Net amount received by the individual is:
£100,000 profit – £49,975 taxes = £50,025

Scenario two: Retaining profits and investing through the business

Here, the business retains profit and pays corporation tax on it.

Corporation tax = £100,000 × 25% = £25,000

Amount available after tax = £75,000

The retained profit is then invested in a corporate investment portfolio. Assume an annual return of 8%.

Investment growth = £75,000 × 8% = £6,000 in the first year

Investment income is typically subject to corporation tax of 25%

Corporation tax on £6,000 × 25% = £1,500

Net investment return = £4,500

Net value of investment after one year: £79,500

While dividends provide a nice fill-up to personal funds, retaining profits for corporate investment results in a significantly higher long-term value: £79,500 plays £50,025. Now add in the power of compounding. Imagine here that the business continues to produce £100,000 a year in surplus profits. Assuming tax rates remain the same, you would receive a total of £150,075 if you took this as a dividend over that three-year period. The corporate reinvestment strategy would produce a different result.

Year 1

Profit: £100,000

Total value at the end of the year: £79,500

Year 2

Starting portfolio: £79,500

Profit added to investment = £100,000 – £25,000 = £75,000

Portfolio value = £79,500 + £75,000 = £154,500

Investment return (assuming 8%): £154,500 × 8% = £12,360

Tax on return: £12,360 × 25% = £3,090

Net return after tax: £12,360 – £3,090 = £9,270

Total value at the end of year 2 = £154,500 + £9,270 = £163,770

Year 3

Starting portfolio: £163,770

Profit added to investment:
£100,000 – £25,000 = £75,000

Portfolio value = £163,770 + £75,000 = £238,770

Investment return (assuming 8%):
£238,770 × 8% = £19,102

Tax on return: £19,102 × 25% = £4,775.50

Net return after tax:
£19,102 – £4,775.50 = £14,326.50

Total value at the end of year 3 = £238,770 + £14,326.50 = £253,096.50

The difference between the sum retained as a dividend, £150,075, and the amount in the corporate investment portfolio, £253,096.50, is substantial and this is after just three years.

Scenario three: Not paying any dividends

Now, here is something else to think about: don't pay any dividends at all. Instead, invest it all in the long-term growth of your business. Create value through your investments and then build upon it. You'll be in good company. Jeff Bezos famously has not paid any dividends since Amazon was founded. This follows Amazon's long-held – and hugely successful – strategy of reinvesting profits back into the business rather than distributing them. Those profits have been ploughed into developing new technologies and entering new markets. This is the fuel that has enabled Amazon to dominate e-commerce, cloud computing and logistics. If the profits had been paid out in dividends, the business may, or may not, have got there in the end with at least some of these markets, but progress would have been a lot slower. I'm convinced that the business would never have been able to dominate as many sectors as it has.

Earlier, I talked about Warren Buffett. I think it might be useful here to look at his story a little more closely because, again, his investing style tells us so much. Most people recognise the name Berkshire Hathaway, the company synonymous with Buffett's success, but how many know that it started out as a significant misstep for him? He had acquired the company in 1965, when it was a struggling textile business. After spending two decades trying to turn it round, he eventually shut down the textiles side and pivoted, using the company as a vehicle to invest in more profitable ventures, including an insurance business. He subsequently said that he had learned many lessons from the textiles misstep. He would, in future, avoid the turnaround trap realising that investing in a struggling business in the hope of changing its fortunes led all too often to poor returns.[15] Connected with this point, he'd made sure that all his subsequent investments were directed towards ventures with high potential for profitability.

All of this has been underpinned by patience and discipline, where his long-term perspective is not swayed by emotional attachments. It was this reinvestment strategy that fuelled his immense success. His investment in the insurance sector, particularly Berkshire Hathaway, was pivotal. Insurance companies collect premiums from policyholders in advance, but pay out claims only later. This gave Buffett a 'float' of millions of dollars: effectively a low-cost, or no-cost, source of capital. He used this float to invest in stocks, bonds and other assets, building significant stakes in companies such as Coca Cola and American Express, all without incurring any debt. Plus, since the insurance business ploughed on, year to year his float was constantly replenished. By the 2020s, Berkshire Hathaway had amassed tens of billions of dollars in insurance float, giving Buffett a virtually limitless pool to deploy in investments.

While any business owner will want to be paid for their hard work, both these examples are powerful indicators of the good sense of letting your profits work hard too. Ask yourself: 'Do I really need to take that dividend? Could it work harder for me elsewhere?'

How much can you invest?

As we all know, *all* investing comes with risk. The obvious one here is that a company can lose the profits it has made through its efforts in its core business by investing them elsewhere. Even if business owners are super cautious, planning carefully and opting to put money into historically stable securities or assets, the market can change. Financial markets can be unpredictable, and downturns will erode the value of any investment portfolio. If the market crashes, you could lose money and not realise anything like the returns you expected. If returns are inconsistent, it can also impact plans to reinvest surplus cash.

Are these risks outweighed by the upside? I would say, yes, very much so. They are certainly better than the 'do nothing' option of waiting it out until a single event that may or may not realise a return. There are steps that can be taken to mitigate the risk too. Given this is a long-term play, it is possible to iron out any potential blips in the strategy. Most importantly, you need to make sure you are in a position to use surplus cash to invest. Then, you need to be careful about how much you use.

Before you decide on any corporate investment strategy, it is crucial to have a clear, and ongoing, idea of your current financial position, to assess how much capital can be allocated to investments. Your business needs sufficient liquidity to cover its day-to-day requirements before funds are allocated elsewhere, particularly for long-term investments. Ideally, there should be a cash buffer in place in case there are any unexpected expenses. Assigning too much to this strategy could leave the core business vulnerable if there was a downturn in the market, or a large, unexpected expense arose, and the investment could not be immediately cashed in. Conversely, if too little is invested, it could hinder the potential to make any meaningful gains. It might be a lot of effort for nothing.

All being well, you will be on top of these details anyway, but make sure you are 100% familiar with your business's cash flow and existing liabilities and with forecasting future expenses.

To help you decide what is right for you, and so you can be strategic about defining the optimum investment amount, I have broken this down to a simple six-step process.

1. Accurately define 'surplus cash'

Surplus cash can be thought of as money in the business bank account that is not required for day-to-day operations, paying back any debt obligations or taking care of any known variable costs. To make this calculation, record the following:

- **Operating expenses.** These are defined as a business's average monthly expenses, which might include fixed costs, such as rent, salaries and utilities, and variable costs. Don't forget to properly account for any seasonal variations in cash flow.

- **Cash flow stability.** Don't rely just on a snapshot in time. Go back and review historic cash flow to check if there is a pattern of months with lower revenue or higher expenses.

- **Debt obligations.** Review all debt servicing requirements, including principal and interest payments. As a side note, don't be tempted to use surplus cash you've identified to clear the decks, by quickly clearing any loans. This can impact on a business's creditworthiness and it might not be an effective use of funds.

- **Planned capital expenditure.** Thought should be given to any planned investments in business assets, such as equipment, facilities or technology, over the next five years which might be funded organically.

After accounting for each of these elements, you should have a clearer idea of any surplus cash that is not required for day-to-day operational or long-term strategic purposes.

2. Establish a liquidity buffer

All businesses need a safety net to protect them against the impact of unexpected expenses or emergencies. This would include equipment breakdowns or the loss of a good client. Any changes that need to be enacted as a result of unforeseen regulatory changes would also be classified as an unforeseen expense. There are three key ways to put this safety net in place:

- **Set a minimum cash reserve.** Consider setting aside a buffer of at least three to six months of operating expenses. The exact sum will depend upon how volatile/vulnerable businesses in a specific sector are known to be.

- **Set a limit for an emergency fund.** This is the fund that will be used for unexpected events. Be realistic here and don't catastrophise, otherwise you can easily fall into the trap of setting far too much aside for events that are unlikely to happen.

- **Factor in market conditions.** Don't forget to consider the impact on the business of an economic downturn. A reasonable cash reserve should be in place to cover a period of reduced sales. This liquidity buffer will give a business instant access to cash when it most needs it, with no need to touch any investment funds.

3. Define investment goals and timescales

Even though the investment will be outside the main day-to-day operations of the core business, it doesn't mean that it should not complement its overall goals and tolerance for risk. The timeline for assessing the potential of investments also needs to align with when the funds will be required. You can define investments in the following ways:

- **Clarify investment objectives.** Document why the business is intending to invest surplus cash. Is it to create an additional income stream or to build a reserve for a future growth strategy? The bulk of the invested funds might not be required until the business owner's projected retirement date, but this needs to be factored in from the start.

- **Fix a time horizon.** Establish the length of time that any surplus cash will be tied up for. This will impact on the nature of the investments being chosen. If liquidity is a priority and the money may be required in less than a year, then the strategy will need to err towards short-term investments. If liquidity is not an issue, a business can pursue longer-term, potentially more lucrative, investment opportunities.

- **Consider your risk tolerance.** If the business owner's risk tolerance is low, then the investment strategy should focus on pursuing low-risk investments. If the tolerance is higher, perhaps because the owner is some years off retirement age, the investment strategy might involve some more high-risk options.

4. External risk assessment

No assessment of external threats can be foolproof – things can change, often unexpectedly – but it is wise to thoroughly investigate the known threats and to have some idea in advance about how to mitigate them. You could try the following:

- **Assess economic and market risks.** Consider the impact of a range of interest rate changes, inflation rates and market volatility. What would it mean financially to your business if, say, inflation was running at 9%?

- **Stress-test for downturns.** Take the worst-case scenario, such as the global financial crisis of 2008–2009, and stress-test what it would have meant if your business had had £XX,000 of surplus cash tied up in investments. Would your cash reserves/liquidity buffer have been adequate during a period this challenging? It may be that you need to adjust your investment figure down a little if the medium-term outlook is less than favourable.

5. Set an investment limit

This step is where you decide on the optimum amount to set aside for investment. This can be achieved in the following ways:

- **Calculate the core reserve.** Using the data gathered from steps 1 through to 3, calculate a reserve level that takes into account operating costs, debt obligations, emergency funds and strategic reserves.

- **Set a maximum investment percentage.**
  Fix an investment range that reflects all
  the factors identified here. A conservative
  approach would be to earmark around
  20–50% of surplus cash for investment.

- **Adjust for growth stage and industry
  factors.** Don't forget to take into account
  the age of the business and the sector it
  operates in. Young businesses will require
  greater investment in the core business
  than established businesses. Companies in
  traditionally volatile industries will need
  to be more cautious too.

6. Monitor and reassess

This is an ongoing programme for the long
term. Even once you have defined the optimum amount to invest externally, don't just
leave it at that. This is, or should be, a dynamic
investment approach. The internal and external environment will change all the time and
business owners should regularly review their
investment portfolio to analyse its performance and re-evaluate if certain investments
are underperforming. The goal is to minimise

risk, which may mean rebalancing the portfolio where necessary. Strategies here include the following:

- **Carry out a quarterly/annual review.** Mark time in the diary to review all investment goals at least once a quarter to see if the amount set aside for investment still aligns with the parameters that were originally set down. Each year, do a deep dive, making a detailed and thorough evaluation of the performance of each investment.

- **Adjust where necessary.** If the situation within the core business and externally changes in any way, adjust investment levels. There may be a call to cash in some investments to replenish cash reserves as required.

- **Rebalance the portfolio.** Be sure to rebalance the portfolio if any changes are made, keeping an eye on risk appetite and liquidity.

Finally, make sure you have a good relationship with your accountant and that they are experienced in corporate investing. As you might imagine, the tax position around the various options can be complex and not always as you'd expect. Interest income and realised gains could be potentially liable for corporation tax, for example, while dividend income from, say, equity exchange-traded funds (ETFs) is not. The amount you'll need to set aside will also depend on a number of different factors, which include the accounting basis adopted by your company and the type of investment involved. These factors can change from budget to budget. You don't want to get caught out. Careful thought also needs to be given to the impact that investments might have on any other reliefs available to, or being used by, business owners. Certain investments will need to be reported on a company's annual return too.

Setting yourself up as a corporate investor

Now you know how much you can afford to invest, the next step is to find the best means to do so. To get started you will need a bespoke share-dealing account. While also known as a business account, the share-dealing account is different from your day-to-day business bank account which you use to pay suppliers and accept fees from clients. This is an investment account, where the entire purpose is to invest. The firms that run these accounts, which include InvestEngine, Interactive Investor, AJ Bell and Lightyear, invest your cash in a range of investments, including the stock market and everything from low-risk bond ETFs and money market funds to equities.

Any director or secretary of a limited company can open this type of account, and there is no limit to how much a company can invest. There are a number of benefits to a bespoke share-dealing account over and above clarifying the tax/dividend situation and making sure businesses get a better rate of return on any cash reserves. These include the following:

- They're easy to set up. You can do it online with as little as £100.
- Business accounts are designed for limited companies and partnerships, although

some platforms will make arrangements for sole traders.

- The money in a business account is easy to access with no exit fees. It can typically be obtained within four to five business days.

- The platforms give users access to hundreds of ETFs or fully managed funds at low cost. Some platforms offer a 'DIY investment portfolio' where users pick their own mix of equities and bonds and a professionally managed account for a small annual fee.

- Investments are automated and can be set for weekly, biweekly or monthly limits.

- Many share-dealing platforms will also help with a legal entity identifier (LEI) number. An LEI is an essential requirement for any business that wants to buy and sell investments. The twenty-character-long code is unique to each business. The platforms will create one for you and it will be free for a set period and then available for a nominal fee after that.

Paying to create one independently would cost around £70 a year.

There are two circumstances where using bespoke platforms like this can come into its own. The first is investing for the short term and the second is squirrelling away cash for long-term, compounded investments.

Let's tackle the short term first. Say, for example, your business routinely sets aside cash to pay the annual corporation tax bill or quarterly VAT expense. If a business owner is prudent, the total sum will be earmarked for the payment well in advance so they don't need to worry about it and it is available on the due date. The upshot of this wholly sensible strategy is that large sums of money are often left untouched in a business account for many months. By using a share-dealing account, the funds can be invested in safe money market short-term securities until they are needed. This would include UK government bonds which are about to mature, short-term deposits with high-credit-quality banks or short-term IOUs from high-credit-quality companies. This is also called commercial paper. Investors will earn a short-term interest rate via the Sterling Overnight Interest Average, or SONIA, which is strongly linked to the Bank of England's bank rate. When the Bank of England raises bank rates, you'll earn a higher rate of interest, and when the bank rate is lowered, investors earn a lower rate of interest. The returns are not spectacular, but this process does lead to a nice and steady source of safe income. It's certainly a lot better than letting a decent amount of cash sit there doing nothing.

The second scenario where these platforms can come in handy is in long-term investing. This would apply to money that is not needed for the day-to-day liquidity needs of a business over long periods of time. In this case, funds can be invested in more risky, or volatile, instruments, such as stocks, which traditionally outperform money market funds.

Once again, being organised and fully aware of your financial position is key. Business owners need to comprehensively understand the liquidity needs of their business so they can decide how much money to put in safe short-term investments to cover those more immediate liquidity needs and how much to invest in riskier and more volatile investments for the longer term.

One thing to be aware of is that while these investment platforms are straightforward and easy to use, business owners are still responsible for understanding the tax implications around their investments, which may vary according to their unique situation. These share-dealing platforms will not automatically deduct the applicable taxes. These sums need to be accurately documented and accounted for and it is up to individual business owners to disclose the cash position on their investments at the end of the tax year. Share-dealing platforms will help with this by providing all the relevant reports and documentation required. This includes a consolidated tax certificate to show the latest income an investment portfolio has earned over a twelve-month period, as well as a CGT report.

If you do decide to work with a share-dealing platform, the usual rules apply. Do your homework and make sure they are the right partner for you. Each one has a different way of working and a different fee structure, and some charge trading commission. Some of the online sites and account opening processes are certainly more user friendly than others. It is worth taking a look at them all individually.

When you decide which platform to go with, you'll need to go through an extensive sign-up process. It is helpful to have the following information to hand:

- The type of legal entity your company is

- Which country your company is incorporated in

- A detailed description of business activities

- Proof of identity for shareholders/directors, such as passports or utility bills

- A copy of the business's memorandum and articles of association

Even if you decide to work with a platform, you do need to be fully informed of the types of investment opportunities on offer, along with the pros and cons of each. In the following chapter, I will take you through the best options for corporate investing.

FOUR

Traditional Options For Corporate Investment

Getting organised is one thing, but it can be a challenge working out where to invest. Business owners will, quite understandably, be nervous about choosing the *right* investment opportunity for their surplus funds. It might feel like a time-consuming activity, hunting out appropriate investments and analysing them to see if they match your risk appetite. It could even be seen as a distraction from managing the primary source of income, pulling attention and resources away from the main revenue-generating operations. (Remember this is one of the outcomes identified as a negative around single transactions.) Plus, if properly pursuing this strategy slowed down growth overall, all the gains would be lost, not to mention there wouldn't be any surplus cash to invest.

To make the most out of this opportunity, a business owner (or a trusted member of their senior team) needs to be excellent at managing operations and have a great understanding of the range of investment opportunities they might try. Once more, a methodical, measured approach is required and, to begin with, that requires market research and due diligence. Mistakes at this stage can prove costly. A little time spent understanding the real potential can save a lot of money and heartache down the line. To get you started, I'll go through the most commonly used corporate investment opportunities, with pros and cons for each. As you will see, each one has its own risk–return profile.

Stocks and shares

Mention the word 'investment' and most people's minds immediately turn to stocks and shares. There's a range of opportunities to invest in quoted companies in various sectors and geographic regions, which can all be used to build a diversified portfolio. A useful resource here is The Motley Fool, which gives you a full and detailed breakdown to the background of every listed company. While a well-managed share portfolio can work well in corporate investing, there are pros and cons. Let's start with the pros.

Potential for high returns

Individuals and businesses invest in the stock market for the same reason: the potential for higher returns. Stocks and shares have historically offered higher returns than leaving cash in the bank, or low-risk bonds, especially over the long term.

Dividend income

Many quoted companies pay dividends to shareholders, providing corporate investors with a fairly reliable source of regular income. This can be a useful passive income, which can be realised without having to sell the shares themselves. Dividend payments are largely predictable too, since they are released on a regular basis, usually quarterly. The steady income can add to a company's health and flexibility.

Hedge against inflation

As already noted, leaving surplus cash in a business bank account is not just wasteful – the value is also eroded over time thanks to inflation. Stocks and shares generally outpace inflation, especially in the long term.

Increased liquidity

When embarking on a corporate investment strategy, it is inevitable that one of the greatest concerns of any business owner will be the possibility of an unexpected expense. If investments can't be quickly sold, this might endanger the business. Publicly traded stocks are more liquid than investments in, say, real estate or private equity. They can be sold quickly and at market value.

Stronger balance sheet/ enhanced valuation

Businesses which hold a good portfolio of stocks and shares are often seen to be more resilient and financially stable. This can be attractive to potential investors and/or creditors.

There are, of course, downsides to any business tying up some of its earnings in stocks and shares. Let's look at the main ones.

Market volatility

The stock market is volatile. Prices fluctuate daily based on a range of factors from economic conditions to geopolitical events, investor sentiment and, of course, the performance of the individually quoted companies. While downturns in stock prices are rarely as extreme as, say, during the financial crisis of 2008–2009, or the bursting of the dot-com bubble in the year 2000, investing in stocks and shares can be a bumpy ride. The good news is that, historically, it works out OK. Over the past 119 years, UK stocks on the FTSE 100 have made annual returns of 4.9% above inflation.[16] (Obviously, past performance is no indicator of future returns.) Problems can arise, though, if the market is in a slump just at the moment a business needs fast access to capital.

Risk of capital loss

There is no guarantee of returns with stocks. Not all stocks will perform well and if the portfolio is not sufficiently diverse, this can be a risky strategy.

Tax implications

Gains from stocks and shares, including dividends, are subject to tax. Any profits will be subject to corporation tax, and businesses may have to pay CGT, depending upon how much of their allowance they have already used in the tax year when investments are sold. These taxes can reduce the net returns of the investment.

Requirement for expertise

Successful investment in stocks and shares requires some knowledge of the market to build a sufficiently diverse portfolio. Businesses may need to invest in expert guidance from financial advisors to help them manage this. This expense will have implications on the overall return.

Funds

An investment in funds, such as a FTSE 100 Index tracker fund, follows the prices of a package of stocks and tracks the ups and downs of the whole index over time. There are hundreds of different indices across the world, which track everything from the market of individual regions to an entire country to large geographical areas such as Europe or the Far East. Within the funds category, there are two basic types of funds. An active fund is run by a fund manager who picks the shares on behalf of their clients. The alternative, a passive fund, will merely buy the whole market or a section of it. As you'd expect, the fees for the former are much higher than the latter.

Again, there are pros and cons to the strategy. We'll start with the pros.

Diversification and risk management

Funds get around some of the downsides of a strategy to invest in individual stocks and shares by providing a more balanced exposure. These packages of investments are inherently diversified because the investment is spread over many assets in a specific market or index, reducing the impact of poor performance by a single one.

Dividend income

If there are dividend-paying companies within a fund, investors will receive dividends directly. How you will receive the dividend will depend upon the fund and its distribution policy. Funds offer two types of shares: income shares and accumulation shares. On the one hand, investors in income shares will receive regular dividend payments as cash, although they can choose to reinvest them. With accumulation shares, on the other hand, dividends are automatically reinvested back into the fund, which is good for anyone pursuing an exponential growth strategy.

Cost-effectiveness

Passive funds generally involve minimal expenses. They also require little input from investors, other than to make the investment itself, which means business owners can get on with the day job.

Increased liquidity

Funds, especially those traded on major exchanges, are generally liquid and can be bought and sold quickly.

Some of the downsides to funds are similar to those to investing in shares. They are subject to market volatility and there is a risk that the investor will lose their stake in the short term if the funds don't perform well. There are a few additional negatives besides. Below are the cons of investing in funds.

Outperformance

Low-cost passive tracker funds are designed to replicate the performance of an index. They'll only ever perform as well as the overall market but never beat it. While active funds do have the potential for outperforming the index, their benefit needs to be weighed up against the larger fees involved.

Currency risk

While investing in international funds, such as S&P 500 or MSCI World Index funds, might feel like an opportunity to realise better returns, it will expose investors to an additional layer of risk. Currency fluctuations can lead to losses, even when the underlying assets in the fund perform well.

Bonds

Investing in bonds can be a viable strategy for any business which prioritises stable and predictable returns. There are a range of options available, from making small loans to other companies through corporate bonds to placing them into Treasury bonds or gilts. The organisation offering the bond is then obligated to pay interest on that loan for a fixed period until its maturity date. During this time, it is also possible to sell a bond on a secondary market, ideally for more than was initially paid. Obviously, bond sellers won't receive interest payments after this date, but it does guarantee a speedier return on investment if needed.

Overall, bonds are generally considered to be a safer option than equities, and some do offer decent returns. A useful resource here is the Hargreaves Lansdown website,[17] which shows that some bonds make a return of up to 14%. They do, however, still have their downsides. As before, let's begin with the upsides.

Stability and predictability

Bonds are less volatile than stocks, which make them appealing as a corporate investment, where capital preservation is key. Income, via regular interest payments, is predictable too. Government bonds, in particular, are felt to be low risk, because they are backed by the government's credit. An alternative – corporate bonds from established companies – typically offers higher yields than government bonds, but this does come with slightly more risk.

Liquidity options

Businesses concerned about committing funds for the longer term can opt for bonds with a shorter maturity time, such as Treasury bills or short-term corporate bonds. Returns will be modest, but again, this is better than doing nothing. Some long-term bonds are, however, quite difficult to sell quickly.

Benefit of balancing portfolio

Bonds generally have an inverse relationship with stocks. When stocks decline, bonds often hold their value. Investors might choose to have both in their portfolio to diversify their interests and minimise risk.

The most obvious downside to bonds is lower returns compared to equities: lower risk equals lower reward. Let's look at the other cons you should consider.

Interest rate sensitivity

Bond prices are interlinked with interest rate changes and the two are highly sensitive to one another. When interest rates rise, bond prices fall, and this works the other way around too. This can pose a risk to investments in long-term bonds, particularly when rates are expected to increase.

Inflation risk

While the stability offered by bonds is welcome, the returns may not be enough to keep pace with inflation, especially in a low-interest-rate economy. If inflation rates rise significantly, the real value of a bond's interest income decreases. This may result in negative real returns. Being locked into long-term bonds can become an issue for businesses when the (already small) benefits are not keeping pace with rising prices. Not only will they be stuck with a bond paying little interest, but also they'll find it difficult to sell it.

Credit risk

Some businesses might try to up the ante by favouring corporate bonds over government ones to get a bit more out of this stable and steady, yet unremarkable, investment. Government bonds are, however, considered safe, and there is a risk here that the issuing corporation may default on their debt obligations. While high-yield, or 'junk', bonds offer temptingly higher returns, they come with a higher risk of default, which could result in a significant capital loss.

Limited growth potential

One of the biggest downsides to bonds is they don't move the dial much. These are income-generating investments, with a fixed return, rather than assets that will grow over time. The performance of the issuing entity matters little beyond its ability to repay debt. Since there will never be any wow factor, also known as significant growth, it does present the question of why to put in all the effort of investing in bonds.

Pension contributions

One of the best-known ways to use up surplus cash in a business is to max out pension contributions. First, we'll consider the pros to this strategy.

Tax advantages

As well as boosting a business owner's retirement savings, this option has two significant benefits tax-wise. The first is that company directors will receive tax relief at their own marginal rate of income tax on any contributions made up to the pension annual allowance, which is the most you can pay into a pension in a single tax year. In the UK, the allowance as of 2024 is £60,000. Any company director who invests money in their pension will also receive corporation tax relief, which will lower their business's overall tax bill. Employer contributions to a pension fund made from pre-taxed income are accounted for as business expenses.

Employee engagement

There is also an option here to make contributions into employee pension funds. These payments also receive full corporation tax relief with no National Insurance payments required. In some sectors in particular, it can be difficult to attract and retain the best talent. A pension scheme that goes above the bare minimum required by law could be enticing for some prospective employees and tip the balance between joining or not joining, or staying and leaving. Who wouldn't want some security for the future? An increase in pension contributions to the existing team can also have a positive impact in terms of greater engagement, improved morale and enhanced retention.

Reduced admin

Investing any excess cash into pension schemes can be a straightforward exercise. It is certainly much less time-consuming than setting up an account to invest in stocks, shares or bonds and then managing them.

Now we'll consider the cons.

Reduced liquidity

The most obvious downside is reduced liquidity. Pension contributions are earmarked for retirement and are therefore inaccessible until the intended recipient reaches retirement age. It is possible to start taking money from a pension from the age of fifty-five (although this rises to fifty-seven from 6 April 2028). There is, however, a catch to this strategy. Once you take taxable money from the plan, which is anything over your tax-free entitlement (25% of the total), your annual allowance will shrink. It will shrink quite drastically too, reducing from £60,000 per year to £10,000. If you are still running the business, this will significantly impact any strategy to max out pension contributions each year.

Potential for lower returns

While the tax benefits of shuffling cash into a pension can't be denied, some pension schemes don't always offer the same potential for growth as other investments, such as forex trading (FX), equities or high-yield bonds. If every spare penny is put into pension schemes, business owners may miss out on opportunities in alternative investments. This point might be especially pertinent to business owners who have a higher risk tolerance.

Property

Buying property is often seen as a stable investment for an individual and a good hedge against inflation, so is it an opportunity for a business with some cash to spare? There is, after all, the dual potential of a rental income and capital appreciation. As with anything in the corporate world, the answer is a little more complex than it might first appear. Let's go through the pros and then cons to break it down.

Rental yields

Businesses have a choice between buying commercial or residential properties, but commercial property usually commands higher rentals than residential. Acquired properties can then be put to work by putting them on the rental market. If long-term tenancy agreements are signed, the rental returns could prove to be a consistent and reliable source of income, which can be used elsewhere for operational expenses or to fund further investments.

Capital appreciation

Historically, real estate appreciates in value over the long term. If property prices rise, so will the equity held in those assets, and the value of well-chosen properties in good locations could significantly rise too.

Volatility hedge

Since property markets are generally less closely linked with stock market movements, real estate investments can be a good hedge against volatility. Businesses can spread the risk by adding property to a diversified portfolio.

Tax benefits

Although the strategies of successive governments have become gradually less friendly to real estate investments, there are still some options to offset certain property-related expenses, such as mortgage interest and maintenance incomes, against rental income.

Control

Business owners can make the decisions about what property to buy and where, the improvements that will be made, tenant selection and rental rates.

Liquidity

The final pro would traditionally have found its way into the con column because property is traditionally seen as an illiquid asset, since it cannot be quickly disposed of if cash is urgently required. The process of selling a property can take many months and, in some cases, years. There are, however, options to streamline this by tokenising the asset. Tokenisation is simply taking something and splitting it up into smaller pieces, each linked to a token. Transactions like this, which involve a multitude of small investors, are a possibility now because the entire transaction, and details of the ownership of every single token, can be stored on blockchain. The property asset is broken down into digital tokens that represent the property with all its rights and obligations. A digital representation of that asset is recorded on blockchain, validating the ownership of that particular asset. An investor can own X% of an asset, up to their personal investment capacity.

Take a house with the asking price of £100,000. Investors might be able to buy a 1,000th of the property by paying £100. If the house is rented, each token promises to pay the owner of the token, say, £0.95 a month. Just like any typical buy-to-let agreement, investors get regular rent yields immediately, rights to vote on decisions regarding property management and sales and, with proper notice to tenants, the right to physically enter and visit a property. Releasing capital tied up in property is always a challenge. Aside from selling it outright, there are other options, such as a second mortgage, reverse mortgage or collateralised loan, but in all cases these are slow, uncertain processes, and high fees or interest are invariably involved. Tokenisation offers the property owner another, potentially quicker and cheaper, option. They could tokenise their property and then leverage the tokens to secure a collateralised loan.

There are also many instances where property might not be the strong investment it first appears to be, particularly when buying a property outright rather than via tokenisation. The most obvious drawback is that business owners are not property managers, and collecting rent and managing tenants can be time-consuming and a needless distraction from the main business. There are other significant disadvantages to this type of investment strategy too.

High initial costs

Buying a property outright involves a substantial investment. The average cost of a residential property in the UK is £299,000[18] and, in October 2024, Stamp Duty Land Tax, a surcharge on additional properties, including buy-to-let, was raised from 3% to 5%. (For properties over £500,000 it rose from 15% to 17%.) It is unlikely that the cash surplus in most businesses will be sufficient to buy a property outright and pay these taxes, which means a commercial mortgage will need to be secured. Business owners therefore need to be certain they can take on this long-term debt. In addition to the mortgage repayments and the initial deposit, there also needs to be provision for legal fees and stamp duty. Plus, ongoing expenses such as maintenance, insurance and property management all need to be allowed for.

Market volatility

While real estate prices generally appreciate over the long term, it does not mean that this type of investment offers a smooth ride. The economic cycle will have a noticeable impact. Investors may find rises in interest rates during a downturn make mortgage costs difficult to manage. When the economy is under pressure, it can also impact rental demand, making it difficult to find tenants prepared to pay the going rate. The illiquidity noted above can make this issue even more acute. If a business needs to sell its real estate quickly to generate funds to support the main business, a declining market will be a barrier.

Tax obligations

While there are some tax benefits to this type of investment, as noted above, there are also a lot of taxes involved when a business buys or sells a property. There is Stamp Duty Land Tax to be paid on purchase, and then, once the property is rented out, there will be income tax or corporation tax due on the rental income, depending upon how the acquisition is structured. When it is eventually time to sell the asset, the owner will most likely be hit with CGT. Again, in the Autumn Budget 2024 there was another increase for landlords. This time, CGT rates were aligned with rates applicable to property sales, with the lower rate rising from 10% to 18% and the higher rate from 20% to 24%.

Regulatory challenges

The current legislative environment does not favour landlords. In their election manifesto the Labour Party, now the Labour government, pledged to 'overhaul' regulation of the private rented sector. At the heart of the Renters' Rights Bill are terms which will give tenants more rights to challenge rent increases and a rule that landlords increase rents only once a year.[19] As well as getting to grips with the ever-changing landlord–tenant rules, property owners will also need to be up to date with health and safety requirements.

Company-to-company investment

One less common, and quite risky, option is to invest surplus cash in other businesses. The thinking here might be that an experienced business owner in a particular sector would be well placed to know if start-ups in the same or a similar sector have a chance to grow and be successful. In this scenario, the business owner would effectively be working as an angel investor. By putting money into this other venture at an early stage, they can earn interest on the amount, then, if the business owner's hunch is right, reap the benefits if the smaller company does well.

Again, let's start with the potential upsides.

Tax incentives

In the UK, business investors can qualify for certain tax reliefs, such as the Enterprise Investment Scheme (EIS) and the Seed Enterprise Investment Scheme (SEIS), if they meet certain qualifying criteria. These are government-backed investment schemes to help get support for early-stage businesses. SEIS offers 50% income tax relief to investors and EIS offers 30%. Any subsequent gains made after holding the shares for more than three years are exempt from capital gains and dividends tax. Thus, if a business sells and the investor makes a profit, they won't pay any tax. To qualify, business owners cannot be an employee or director of the firm they are investing in or, together with their associates (business partners, spouses or direct relatives), hold more than 30% of the company.

High growth potential

There is no guarantee of success with any start-up – far from it. If it does take off, however, it could make remarkable returns for early investors. Some angel investments have reportedly achieved ten times the amount in returns. A handful of megastars have made even more. If a start-up has that magic ingredient that inspires customers, it can scale rapidly.

Synergies

If one business invests in another in a complementary market, it can give them both a competitive advantage. Each business can share any advances or integrate any improved systems made by the other party into their own offer. It basically doubles the chance of staying ahead of industry trends.

As is probably abundantly clear by now, this option is at the riskier end of the investment spectrum. Let's look at why.

High failure rate

Most people are familiar with the fact that a large number of start-ups never make it past the first few years. The true figure, statistically, is that 60% of small businesses never make it beyond the first three years of life.[20] The chances that any angel investor will lose their initial stake are high. In fact, it is more likely they will lose it all than they won't. Even if the business they've invested in does stay the course, the chances that there will be any return on the investment are tiny. As per the theme of this book, the odds of a single transaction are long. Just 2% of these types of investments will exit, either being bought by a trade buyer or undergoing an IPO, within five years. Some sectors are more risky than others. Anything from live events to clothing to cafes is more likely to fail, whereas businesses in nursing and care services, healthcare and property development have better odds. Even so, this is a risky investment strategy and the chances of success are low.[21]

Valuation

The risks are apparent from the start, especially for novices. Angel investing requires some prior knowledge of venture funding, growth potential and valuation. It is difficult to accurately value a start-up, even for supposed experts.

Start-ups have little, or no, financial history and their products are yet to be proven in the market. An investor could easily overpay, meaning that even if the business did stay the course, they would not receive a reasonable rate of return in comparison to the risk of making the investment in the first place.

Illiquidity

Start-ups are looking for a long-term commitment from their investors. There is little chance of getting any money out until the company exits, which can be five years or more in the future, if ever.

Partnership relationship

It is rare (and also not prudent) for an angel to invest in a start-up and to simply walk away, never speaking to the start-up principals again until the hoped-for exit. Any angel investment is predicated on partnership. The start-up will value insights and advice from a more experienced operator who will help shape future products, services and strategies. It is in the investor's interest to share their knowledge too, since this will help the start-up grow. All of this does, however, take time and will inevitably be a distraction from the day job.

Dilution risk

It's great news if the investment in a start-up seems to bear fruit and the new business begins to grow at pace, yet this can also be an issue for early investors. To maintain the growth, the start-up may need to raise successive rounds of funding. Early investors will have to choose between stumping up more cash, which could negatively impact the core business, or seeing their initial stake diluted by subsequent investors.

There is one further option I would like to suggest and that is FX, which has the potential to be the star of your corporate investing portfolio. It is more risky than many of the traditional investments listed here, and also quite complex to understand for beginners, so I have devoted the next chapter to FX trading.

FIVE

FX: Shooting For The Stars

When building a business, it's normal to rely on the usual suspects for growth: good, reliable products, better marketing, more aggressive sales efforts and maybe a few strategic discounts. Get the mix right and tactics like this usually guarantee decent results, at least in the short term and as long as you keep up the momentum. It is the same with investments. As I've shown in the previous chapter, there are a number of sensible options in corporate investing. While each has its pros and cons, they all have the capacity to help you build a decent nest egg and are infinitely better ways of securing your financial future than hoping for the best with an eventual sale of your business.

What, though, if you wanted something a bit more ambitious? What if you've fully bought into the idea of *exponentially* increasing your wealth, creating stratospheric growth in your financial future? If there is one thing that I have learned through a lifetime spent building and investing in businesses, it is that taking the safe option – ie doing the same as everyone else – is never the answer to make the gains I want to make. I'm fully behind the idea of corporate investing, but the key to any successful strategy is to take a good concept and then seek out ways to make it *even stronger*. My goal is to help you propel your returns so they are double, or even triple, maybe even more, than you ever hoped for.

To design my own market-beating strategy, I started by doing some research. The best place to begin seemed to be to scrutinise the super-rich and City traders: how did they make such huge gains? What was their secret? Whatever it was, I wanted to play their game. The answer soon came back loud and clear: FX. This is the process of currency trading where you make money from money. Traders predict the outcome of the rise and fall from one currency against the other and make money out of the price fluctuation. It's a huge operation, with up to US$6.6 *trillion* traded every day.[22] Successful FX traders can make gains of 1% to 10% every month with this strategy.[23] Remember the discussion about compounding earlier? If you managed to achieve 1%, or even half that, at the lower end of the scale but invested back the proceeds, you would begin to build up a respectable war chest. In this market, hourly, or even minute-by-minute, fluctuations can be leveraged to grow wealth at an accelerated pace as each pound of profit is reinvested into new FX opportunities.

The basics: How does FX trading work?

The real boom in FX trading for people like you or me began in the late nineties. Before this, this type of trading was practised exclusively by major banks and big City institutions. Then, along came personal computers and the internet and suddenly everyone was able to join in. Why did tech make all the difference and open the market to all? The main reason is that there is no single physical place or exchange where we can buy and sell currencies. The FX market is everywhere – and nowhere. It is a global, decentralised market for currency trading that runs twenty-four hours a day, five days a week. (If you'd like to be specific on the hours, it is open from 9pm GMT on Sunday and closes at 8pm GMT on Friday.) This makes FX trading the most liquid and accessible financial market in the world, which, as you might imagine, vastly increases the opportunities to grow your money.

How, though, does it work? In FX, trading currencies are quoted in pairs and the process involves simultaneously buying one currency while selling another. Each country has its own, unique, three-letter code to make it quickly identifiable. Some of the most recognisable pairings are, say, the euro (EUR) against the US dollar (USD) or the British pound (GBP) versus the Japanese yen (JPY). Each of these pairs represents the exchange rate between two currencies. Other currencies include Swiss francs (CHF), Canadian dollars (CAD), Australian dollars (AUD) and New Zealand dollars (NZD).

There is a bit of lingo to be learned, but it is worth spending the time to get to grips with it. It will make the process far simpler in the long run. Thus, the **base** currency is the first currency in the pair and always found on the left. Think here of the EUR in the EUR/USD pairing. The second currency in this example, the dollar, is known as the **quote** currency. If you buy EUR/USD as a currency pair, you are **buying** the EUR as the base currency and **selling** the USD as the quote currency. If the value of the euro increases against the dollar, you can sell the position for a profit. Likewise, if the euro weakens against the dollar, you will make a loss.

The base currency is always equal to one, while the quote currency is equal to the current quote price of the pair. This shows you how much of the quote currency it will cost to buy one unit of the base. To put numbers on this, if, say, the EUR/USD is trading at 1.43121, this means €1 is worth US$1.43121. The exchange rate is the amount of the quote currency, in this case dollars, that is equal to one unit of the base currency, or euros.

It is possible to buy and sell any currency, and there are hundreds of different combinations to choose from. To make it a little easier to follow, FX trading is broken down into three distinct categories: major pairs, minor pairs and exotic pairs. Seven pairs, each including a dollar, are considered to be major pairs: EUR/USD, USD/JPY, GBP/USD, USD/CHF, USD/CAD, AUD/USD and NZD/USD. When it comes to minor pairs, this category includes two major currencies where neither of them is the US dollar. Examples here would be GBP/EUR and AUD/JPY. An exotic pair will include one major currency against another from an emerging economy, such as the Turkish lira (TRY) or Hungarian forint (HUF).

There are a few other terms you will need to get to grips with, which may sound a bit confusing at first, but you'll quickly get used to them. One is a **pip**. This simply means a one-digit movement in the fourth decimal place of a currency pair. If, as per the example above, the EUR/USD moves from US$1.43121 to US$1.43131, then it has moved a single pip. A price movement at the fifth decimal place is a **pipette**. Another term to know is **lot**. In FX trading, currencies are traded in lots. Since price movements are generally miniscule, perhaps just one pip, lots are usually quite large. A standard lot is 100,000 units of the base currency. Also be aware of **spread**. The spread is the difference between buy and sell prices.

What, then, moves the markets? In other words, what factors will influence the price difference between the pairs? The first element is straightforward: good old supply and demand. If the demand for one currency is higher than for the other in the pair, then the price of that currency will rise.

What any FX trader needs to be familiar with are the factors that impact supply and demand. Here, we can't ignore the role of central banks, which have a significant influence over the price of the currency in their own markets. Or at least try to do so. They've got a box of tricks to keep currencies stable, and the dominant choice is almost always to raise or lower interest rates. When interest rates go up, the currency should increase in value, mostly because it attracts foreign investors. Another, relatively recent, phenomenon is quantitative easing, where more money is injected into the economy during an economic slowdown. The intended outcome is that a currency's price will drop thanks to the increased supply. Central banks are supported by governments in their endeavours, using changes to tax rates and public spending to calm currencies.

How much – or how little – a country trades on the international stage will have an impact too. Countries with a trade deficit – that import more goods than they export – have to buy the currencies of their trading partners to pay for imported goods. This means the currency of regions with trade deficits are worth less than those in the opposite position with a trade surplus. Don't discount the impact of market sentiment in driving currency prices either. Good news always increases demand for the currency of a region and vice versa: bad news can see demand drop. There can be a bit of a snowball effect here too. If FX traders perceive that a currency is firmly moving in a particular direction, they will follow suit, encouraging more traders to do the same. This herd behaviour can exacerbate price movements.

Pros of FX trading

Before we look at how to get started in FX trading, let's look at the pros for corporate investors. This is basically the small print but a bit more informative.

Investment opportunity

The FX market is the largest, and most liquid, in the world. If you have bought into the idea of making better use of surplus cash, it makes sense to consider this as an option. Investing in foreign currencies offers access to a wide range of markets, many of which would be impossible to reach through traditional equities or bonds. The liquidity also means it is possible to quickly enter and exit positions, so investors can capitalise on short-term movements in currencies.

Hedging against currency risk

One area where FX trading can come into its own is businesses that trade on an international basis. As anyone who operates a business that trades across multiple countries will know only too well, fluctuations in exchange rates can have a big impact on the profitability, or otherwise, of each sale. FX trading offers hedging options, such as forward contracts to lock in exchange rates and stop any last-minute surprises. A US seller of, say, high-end furniture with a growing

client base in the UK might use a forward con-
tract to lock in the GBP/USD exchange rate.
By doing this, fluctuations in the pound won't
negatively impact revenue when invoices are
paid and need to be converted to dollars. This,
in turn, is a useful tool in managing cash flow.

Diversification

It can pay to diversify an FX portfolio; however, since currency movements can be fluid,
traders need to be vigilant. Currency markets
are influenced by different, often far broader
yet also more visible, factors than stocks and
bonds. Changes to interest rates, political insta-
bility and shifts in the national economy can
all have an impact, to name but a few. The
most successful FX traders keep a keen eye
on world events so they can anticipate which
way currencies might shift. Aside from external
events, there are some basic rules that apply
too. Some regions can seem relatively stable,
currency-wise, for long periods of time, so the
returns will not be exceptional. Currencies from
emerging markets like Brazil or India, however,
hold more potential for higher returns because

they are going through periods of exceptional economic growth.

Ease

It is easy to open an FX trading account. There are various online services and it can take just half an hour to get going, with as little as £100 to begin with. Since it is a 24/5 market, it is possible to manage the account out of hours, so it doesn't have to be a distraction from the main business either. Traders can get in and out of positions at any time, and the ability to sell short a currency is a given, which might not always be the case with other markets, such as stocks.

As you become more experienced, you'll discover a number of different trading styles, all of which you can vary depending upon whether your investment strategy is built around a short- or long-term outlook. Below, I have highlighted five types of holding positions, listed in order from short- to long-term outlooks. Again, it is worth familiarising yourself with the terms.

1. **Scalping**: Opened and closed rapidly, with the goal of taking a series of small profits

2. **Day trading**: Opened and closed within the same day

3. **Swing trading**: Highs and lows are anticipated, with trades placed on the expectation of price reversals

4. **Trend trading**: Pursuing an overall trend

5. **Position trading**: Held for long periods, weeks, months or even years

Fees

The FX market is decentralised, so there are no exchange or clearing fees. The costs of making the trade are priced in. The only exception to this is if the trade is via an electronic communications network, which I will go into in more detail shortly. What is also attractive is the flexibility of lot size. While a standard lot is 100,000 units of base currency, it is possible to trade mini lots (10,000 units) or micro lots (1,000 units).

Cons of FX trading

FX trading can be a risky business, so you need to know the downsides as well as the upsides.

Risk

The elements that make FX trading an attractive option also make it a risky one. The market is known for its volatility, as it is fuelled by a range of factors such as economic shifts, political manoeuvring and central bank policies. This volatility drives opportunities for profit, but the opposite is also true. A sudden market downturn or political coup in an emerging economy can lead to a rapid devaluation in currency. Any investor who has failed to see the warning signs will find themselves holding substantial losses. For the corporate investor, this can be exceptionally off-putting because losses could impact the financial stability of the core business. This is why it is so important to go through the processes outlined in chapter three – so sufficient money is always available for day-to-day operations.

Lack of regulation

Regulatory oversight of the FX market is patchy, and this includes brokers. Traders will be safe opening accounts with established brokerage firms, regulated in their home country, because they come with the safety net of segregated funds, negative balance protection and a compensation fund. Some offshore brokers, however, don't offer these kinds of protections. What can add an extra layer of confusion is that some of the larger brokerage firms have multiple offices across the world. Each one is governed by a different set of regulations. The protections put in place by some regulators will protect only those investors who live in the immediate jurisdiction. Again, this is why doing proper due diligence ahead of time is crucial.

Dividends

While investing in shares is not as dynamic as FX, the option does at least offer the opportunity to receive dividend payments. This is not something offered in currency trading. I should add that this can be tempered at least partly by a strategy known as a 'carry trade'. Here, a pair is bought where the base currency has a high-interest yield and the quote one, a low yield. The investor can then benefit from the interest rate differential: the interest earned from the high-yielding pair minus the interest paid from selling the low-interest one.

How to trade FX

For beginners, the best advice would always be to start gently while you get to know the layout of the market. The first thing to decide upon is the currency pairs you want to trade and the time of day you'll open and close your positions. When getting started, most people choose the major pairs: the USD and one other, such as GBP or EUR. There are a few advantages to doing so for the novice. This is a popular trade, so it guarantees a high volume of sellers in the market. Orders will also be executed quickly at competitive prices. The major pairs are a little more predictable too because it's unlikely there will be any unnerving sudden price spikes. Once you've found your feet, you might like to move on to minor and exotic pairs. While there will be less liquidity, they will be volatile and there is the potential for some significant wins (and losses too, obviously). On timing, the recommended starting point for the novice trader is during the overlapping hours between the London and New York stock exchanges. This is when the FX market is at its most liquid, with increased volatility, so there are better chances to take a position that might see some movement.

There are two options for trading FX. The first is to trade on the spot market. The spot market gives a live price for the FX pair you've chosen, to buy or sell the currencies immediately. Alternatively, you can trade on the futures market, based on what you believe the future value of the pair may become. The price is based on futures contracts, where traders agree to buy or sell a currency pair at an agreed price for a date in the future.

When it comes to making trades, there are also two options: you can take a do-it-yourself approach or let the machines take charge by letting computer programs do the heavy lifting. I'll tackle the DIY approach first. To get started, you'll need to open an FX trading account with a brokerage firm which has the trading interface to access the market. This is basically a hub where they execute trades, analyse market data and manage accounts. You'll find a number of brokers online, who will have their own bespoke tools and resources and many of whom will offer simplified interfaces and tutorials for beginners. These accounts are simple to open, with only a small cash deposit. Some services will even let you open a demo account, so you can see what it is like to trade and follow price movements. This can help you refine your trading strategy before you do it for real. If you want some tips on how the experts do it, try a platform like eToro, which lets beginners copy the trades of experienced traders.

To get started, you'll need a maintenance margin. This makes sure there are sufficient funds in your account to cover any moves in your position. It is wise to monitor and review this amount because if the balance falls below the maintenance level, there is a risk that the position will be closed. This is particularly pertinent at a time of high volatility in the chosen pair.

As I mentioned earlier, it is useful to understand the lingo, but you'll pick a lot up once you get going. Another useful element to get to grips with is orders, which help you manage risk. Stop-loss orders and take-profit orders (also known as limit orders) are instructions to automatically close a position when it reaches a predetermined level. A stop-loss order does exactly that, closing out a trade to minimise losses when a trade is at a point where the price is worse than the current market level. Conversely, a take-profit order is an implicit instruction to close out a trade when it is better than the current market level. It locks in price targets.

If this all sounds overwhelming, it is no big surprise. This is why algorithmic trading was invented and computers do it all for you. In the past, algorithmic trading was the preserve of institutional investors and hedge fund managers, but it's now available to ordinary investors via algorithmic platforms and brokers. In fact, this is the basis for one of my businesses, Elect Holdings. I set it up because I wanted to emulate what Warren Buffett had done with Berkshire Hathaway, and this seemed the most efficient way of doing it.

The way these programs work is simple. Once you've inputted a precise overview of the trading strategy you want to follow, algorithms can quickly analyse vast amounts of market data, accurately identify the most compelling trading opportunities and then execute the trades that most closely follow the instructions.

Using algorithmic platforms makes a lot of sense. They can analyse a lot more data than we can, much more quickly, to identify the best prices to buy or sell. Being automated, there is no chance of 'fat fingers' making a mistake and executing the wrong trade. Overall, this adds up to a more efficient trading strategy and better returns. In the interests of transparency, I should add there are some potential downsides. The first is related to the instructions that you input in the set-up phase. If you aren't accurate in the parameters you set down, it is possible that you'll lose more than you've set aside for the corporate investment strategy. The second point is closely related to the first. If you make a higher number of simultaneous trades, at speed, and it is not going your way, the losses will compound and quickly get out of hand.

If you feel the algorithm pros outweigh the cons, a quick Google search will show you that there are *a lot* of platforms to choose from. My advice would be to experiment with a few platforms to find which interface best suits you and is easiest to navigate. If you are the analytical type, which we all should be to a certain extent, experiment with the analysis and risk management tools. Consider too whether the platform you favour has both mobile and web access. If you are checking trades at different points of the day and night, it is sometimes more convenient to use your smartphone to check on open positions.

As you become more confident, the best guidance is to design a strategy and stick with it. Just as per the advice about choosing traditional investments, you should be forensically measured about FX trading. When you choose your preferred pairing, do some background reading to make sure you understand both currencies. Actually, no, do *a lot* of background reading. The goal is to know and understand the main economic and political forces that might have an impact.

Everything you are doing should be designed to take the emotions out of the process. It's easy to say that you need to remain calm and methodical, but it's quite another thing to achieve this when you are presented with significant gains or losses. If you have a clear trading plan, and stick to it, it will stop you making irrational decisions based on what has just happened. There's a City mantra which says 'cut your losses and let your profits run' and it is not bad advice. It's a mistake to take profits as soon as they appear (not least because you'll lose the benefits of compounding). Similarly, if you are too cautious and walk away at the first negative sign because you don't want to make a loss, you will also reduce your chances of making any meaningful progress. Trading FX is, or should be, a learning process. The only way to learn, though, is to not get carried away and instead analyse each transaction with a cool eye. Think about what worked and what didn't and use the information as the foundation for future trades.

SIX

Invest Smarter:
Let Your Company
Build Your Legacy

The goal of this book is not only to help you move away from the single-transaction dilemma but also to help you make the most out of the money you have today. As I have already shown, simply taking all your surplus cash out as dividends is not tax efficient and will, in fact, result in a loss of capital compared to deploying it in different ways. In this final chapter, I'd like to bring this all together by illustrating how effective your money can be and how you can make it even more effective while reducing risk down to your tolerance levels.

While corporate investing is the answer to generating a steady and consistent growth in your financial status so you can reap the rewards today and not at some distant time in the future (or never), you need to be measured in your approach. As I have already clearly outlined, some of the investment options on offer do carry a degree of risk and some more so than others. You are, therefore, strongly advised to consider diversifying your corporate investment portfolio. Diversification is the cornerstone of sound financial planning. If you invested all of your surplus cash into one of these assets, it would expose you to the risk of losing everything, which is obviously not an acceptable outcome in any financial portfolio and certainly not with something as important as your day-to-day livelihood. Spreading investment funds across various asset classes lets you try great high-growth opportunities while greatly reducing risk and improving the potential for steady returns. It also adds some protection against certain market-specific risks.

Diversifying your investment portfolio

Diversification, like all financial strategies, requires resources and expertise to get right, and you will need to carefully monitor your portfolio. It begins with being familiar with your situation as it is now. Everyone is different, with different short-, medium- and long-term objectives and different risk appetites, and it is crucial that you are familiar with all the parameters that impact your investment decisions.

I'd like to share a practical framework that you can use to assess your position. I have grouped the information you need to know into categories that will help you make the necessary decisions about your corporate investment portfolio. Take a little time considering your answers to each of the following questions.

1. Financial returns

The first step is to determine the profitability and growth potential of the investment you are planning to make over a defined period. You should consider the following key parameters:

- **Initial investment**: What will be your starting amount after accounting for taxes or fees? Will you be using pre-tax or post-tax profits?

- **Growth rate**: What is the average annual-ised rate of return among your preferred assets? Is this rate still realistic based on historical data and current market conditions?

- **Time horizon**: What is the duration of the investment (eg one year, five years, ten years)?

- **Additional contributions**: Will you be making periodic injections of profits or capital? When will you be making these contributions and what is the anticipated amount?

The information here will help you analyse the potential wealth growth over the investment period. In your calculations, it is helpful to separate the returns from the initial capital and any top-ups so you can make a more detailed comparison of returns.

2. Risk assessment

As the saying goes, the value of your investments can go down as well as up. You need to understand your tolerance for risk and how you would manage any losses. The key parameters you need to consider here are:

- **Volatility**: When weighing up assets, what is the degree of price fluctuation for each asset class?

- **Risk management**: Are you familiar with tools such as stop-loss orders, diversification and hedging?

- **Exposure**: What percentage of total capital are you prepared to risk in any single investment? (A prudent approach might be to limit this to 5–10% for high-risk strategies.)

- **Historical performance**: Have you analysed the past performance data of your preferred assets to gauge risk levels?

This exercise will help you properly evaluate the probability of losses versus potential gains. You could score each of your preferred assets according to whether the risk is high (speculative or highly volatile), moderate (managed risk with diversification or hedging) or low (stable assets with minimal downsides).

3. Liquidity

Your business still needs to operate on a day-to-day basis and things don't always go to plan, however carefully they are managed. You need to assess how quickly and easily any of your investments could be converted into cash without significant loss. The key parameters to consider here are as follows:

- **Asset type**: How many liquid assets, such as cash, stocks or FX trading, will be in your portfolio? How many illiquid assets, such as real estate or private equity, are you planning to include?

- **Time to liquidate**: How many days or weeks are required to sell or withdraw funds from each of your preferred assets?

- **Market conditions**: What is the availability of buyers/sellers and exit options for each asset? What impact will adverse market conditions have on liquidity?
- **Penalties or restrictions**: Are there any fees or time-based penalties for early liquidation?

Liquidity can be scored on a similar basis to risk, on a scale from high to low. High means assets that can be sold or accessed instantly without penalties, moderate means assets requiring some time or costs to liquidate, and low applies to long-term or restricted assets.

This is an analytical approach that will help you decide on the assets that best suit your risk appetite and offer the required level of liquidity should the business need access to ready money. As with the earlier assessment, this is an ongoing process. The weighting of your investment options can and should be adjusted over time, especially when particular growth opportunities arise. Again, this should all be part of a careful planning process with all the risks factored in. This is key to managing risk and ensuring consistent returns.

Weighting your portfolio

Now you have all the information at your fingertips, you will be equipped to make decisions about how you'd like to weight your portfolio. While I have advocated strongly for FX as one of the most effective forms of corporate investment, you might like to deploy some of your capital elsewhere at the same time. An investment in the currency markets can be balanced against safer and more 'reliable' investments such as bonds and topping up your pension.

The goal here is to hold a balance of lower-risk assets like bonds and higher-risk options like FX and stocks and shares. The latter will help your portfolio to grow quickly, while the former offer less spectacular returns but should act as a cushion against any volatility. Sure, you could risk it all in the FX market, but you might find it quite difficult to sleep at night.

Your personal risk appetite will have a bearing on the diversification you build into your corporate investment portfolio, as will the time horizon you anticipate holding your individual investments for.

Generally, diversification is expressed as a percentage. Let's say you think FX is just too risky for the moment and instead choose a combination of stocks and bonds. Here the investing styles would be expressed as **aggressive** (90% stocks/10% bonds), **moderate** (70% stocks/30% bonds) and **conservative** (50% stocks/50% bonds).

The higher the stock percentage, the greater the growth potential, but it will also be the more volatile choice. Meanwhile, the higher percentage of bonds will increase stability, but you will be facing lower long-term returns.

You may prefer to begin more cautiously with your investment strategy and build the risk element up over time by introducing riskier, but high-growth, options as you feel more confident. These decisions should always be made after thoroughly investigating all the options and returning to your initial plan to see what, if anything, has changed.

Whatever happens, the balance of assets you invest in is not a one-time calculation. A diversified portfolio requires active management. To stick with the shares and bonds example here, imagine that, all being well, the stocks you've invested in have a strong run. This will result in the equity side of the portfolio growing more quickly than forecast. You will then have a decision to make. Do you shift some of the earnings into bonds to maintain the preferred asset allocation? Financial experts recommend rebalancing portfolios when an asset class moves more than 5% or 10% from the original target. This is certainly something to consider, especially if you want to stick closely to your carefully identified risk tolerance and goals. You should also regularly revisit your overall asset mix to make sure it fits in with your timeline. As you get closer to retirement, for example, it might be wise to reduce the risk profile.

There are some possible downsides to diversification. It can dilute returns, for example, especially if you are far more cautious than you perhaps need to be. Also, while diversification is highly recommended, it is not foolproof. One of the most common mistakes is to diversify too much. It might sound like a good idea to spread the risk across multiple asset classes and get the best of all worlds, but you can go too far. Many of the risk factors for different assets overlap, so it makes little sense to push up your investment costs in the name of a fully diversified portfolio. Besides, if the performance of each asset is similar, they won't be offering the diversity you are looking for. Another unintended outcome of a diversified portfolio is that in some scenarios seemingly diversified investments respond in exactly the same way to market stimuli, such as a downturn. Obviously, this reduces the effectiveness of the diversification strategy.

On the whole, the recommendation would always be to look to protect your money, so diversification is still the sensible option. Planning is key here, as is monitoring the progress of all investments. If you are looking to invest in a few different assets, think about how to keep costs down. I've mentioned brokers a few times in this book. When making your choice about which platform to use, factor in your diversification choices. Some brokers offer the opportunity to invest in multiple assets, which might be handy. It also makes sense to keep everything together so you can easily move assets around if your appetite changes.

In the final section of this chapter, I would like to look at one more way to make the most out of your corporate investment strategy: asymmetric investing. This is how you can greatly increase your investment returns among your more volatile assets like FX and stocks and shares.

Asymmetrical risk versus reward: Keeping losses small

When embarking on an investment strategy for the first time, you'll most likely be inclined to dream big. Imagine, for example, you've decided to allocate a percentage of your investment money to FX. When starting out as an FX trader, you might think, *If I win at each trade, I'll be quids in.* There's nothing wrong with dreaming big – I'd encourage it – but it is the way you achieve those dreams that counts. Forget about pulling out all the stops to win each trade or investing only in stocks that you are sure will soar in value. That's not the approach, or mindset, you need. Besides, you won't ever win in this way, so don't even think about it. No, what you need to do is aim for a few investments where the gains are so significant they wipe out all the losses and make meaningful returns.

The process to achieve this is via a risk–reward ratio trade, more commonly known as an asymmetrical trade. Here, the potential upsides, or returns, significantly outweigh the possible downsides, or risks.

Once again, I'm borrowing from the playbook of the world's top players in the markets, in this case Paul Tudor Jones. Tudor Jones is one of the most financially successful investors in the world. He is said to be worth more than US$8 billion and his firm manages US$13 billion in assets.[24] He cites asymmetrical trading as the key to succeeding on his path towards the big profits and has perfected what he calls the five-to-one strategy. In an interview with motivational speaker Tony Robbins, he said:

'Five to one means I'm risking one dollar to make five. What five to one does is allow you to have a hit ratio of 20%. I can actually be a complete imbecile. I can be wrong 80% of the time, and I'm still not going to lose.'[25]

Asymmetrical risk is built on that truism of every investment that in every trade, every investor is subject to one of two possible outcomes: they'll either make money or lose money. Success as an investor is predicated on balancing those options so you make money more times than you lose it. The further you tip the scales towards making money, the better off you'll be. Asymmetrical trading involves risking a relatively small amount of capital, with the potential to achieve disproportionately high gains. It's well suited to volatile markets like FX and stocks and shares.

At this point, you may be thinking: *Isn't this a bit risky?* After all, in the previous chapters I have counselled strongly that you should be cautious about how you invest the surplus cash in your business. The goal here is to generate growth in revenue and create a nest egg, after all. Asymmetrical trading is, however, a much more measured approach. You don't need to bet the farm to win big. In reality, this strategy is geared towards taking a lower amount of risk. You will not only be protecting your account from getting out of control by setting strict stop limits, but you will also be positioning yourself to make decent returns. Turn this on its head and think about traditional investing strategies. Most people go all in for 'safe' assets in the hope their capital will rise 10% in a good year, 20% if it is a great one. Since all investments carry at least some degree of risk, this seems to me to be risking a lot to make very little. It's the opposite to asymmetrical investing, which is risking a little to make a lot.

It might help to break the process down a little, to set your mind at rest. You'll need to start by calculating your risk appetite relative to your return. To illustrate how this works, I will use the example of an FX trade, but it works in largely the same way with shares, although I will add some further clarification later in this chapter.

The process involves taking the sum of your whole trading account as a starting point. Let's say the value of your entire investment portfolio is £10,000. When analysing your risk, your final result will be judged against the return on this total sum. In other words, you are looking at a return on £10K, not a return on an individual investment. This will significantly amplify your potential for success. Now, you may think that if you traded £100 in FX and made £100, you would have doubled your investment. In this context, though, this is not true. You would have increased your £10,000 equity by 1% to £10,100.

Let me walk you through the process of making the £100 FX investment work for you. Stop-loss orders are handy tools in an asymmetrical risk strategy. Once you decide your risk appetite, or how much money you are willing to lose on a trade, you can build this into your trading plan.

Here are our assumptions:

Total portfolio size: £10,000

Amount to be invested in FX: £100

Trading leverage: 10:1
(common in FX trading)

Currency pair: EUR/USD

Entry price: 1.1000

Target price: 1.1200
(potential gain of 200 pips)

Stop-loss price: 1.0950
(potential loss of fifty pips)

With a £100 investment and leverage of 10:1, the value of the position the trader controls is calculated as follows: position size = investment × leverage; therefore £100 × 10 = £1,000.

The investor is therefore trading as though they have £1,000 in the market, magnifying both potential gains and losses.

Now to calculate the risk.

Remember, the stop loss is set at 1.0950. Each pip movement is calculated as follows: value per pip = position size × pip size; therefore £1,000 × 0.0001 = £0.10.

If it all goes badly, the total loss if the price hits the stop loss is: loss = value per pip × pips lost; therefore £0.10 × 50 = £5.

If, however, things go the other way and the investment reaches the target price, there is a different picture. Using the same pip value of £0.01, our calculation would be: profit = value per pip × pips gained; therefore £0.10 × 200 = £20.

To determine the risk–reward ratio, compare the potential loss to the potential gain: risk–return ratio = potential loss; therefore £5 = 1:4 and the potential gain is £20.

In this scenario, the investor is risking £1 for every £4 of potential profit. They can be wrong three times out of four and still come out even. It is up to you to define what you believe to be the right risk–return ratio for you. You might opt for a 1:4, or 1:5 like Paul Tudor Jones. You could go even higher and risk £1 to make £15.

In all cases, by increasing the initial stake, the potential gains and losses scale proportionally.

To illustrate this, we'll use a £500 investment at the same leverage, which would therefore control a position worth £5,000.

Value per pip: £5,000 × 0.0001 = £0.50

Loss at fifty pips: £0.50 × 50 = £25

Profit at 200 pips: £0.50 × 200 = £100

Even traders like Paul Tudor Jones will make the wrong call. They can even be wrong lots and lots of times. As per the five-to-one example he gives above, however, he knows that if he loses US$1, he can still risk another US$3 and be in profit. A range of investments with high reward–risk opportunities will have maximum upsides.

It is worth noting that while you could also use this asymmetric strategy for stocks and shares, it does require you to be a little more astute about the process. True asymmetric opportunities are harder to find in this context. (If it was easy, everyone would be doing it, right?) Sometimes, you will need to hold on for the long term, as it can take time to turn that £1 into £5 or £10. You may even have to sit through some rocky moments before you hit your target.

The key here is to do your homework so you know what you are getting into. I would even go as far as to write down the reasons why you are investing in a particular stock and why you feel it is such a sure-fire thing. That way, if it veers off course, away from your predetermined parameters, you can cut your losses. An extreme example might be a newly floated self-driving, electric van maker, who you believe will revolutionise the home delivery market. If legislation got in the way of its ambitions and the rule-makers blocked progress, the business may decide to pivot away from its initial premise. It might start building hybrid vans with no self-driving ability at all. In this case, the idea that this business will *revolutionise* the home delivery market is invalid. There are plenty of other, similar companies operating in the market it has pivoted into. The asymmetric advantages are gone, therefore, and it is best to look elsewhere.

Sometimes, these types of asymmetric share investments pay off extremely well. One of the most famous examples would be hedge funder David Tepper, who made US$7 billion of profit (yes, *billion*) in the 2008 banking crisis. The former Goldman Sachs junk bond trader took the view that the US government would not let banks such as Citigroup and Bank of America collapse, even though the stock price indicated that most traders thought otherwise. He was, of course, right. When the banks were bailed out, the stock price soared. For relatively little risk, he grabbed a slot at the top of the league of Wall Street's biggest earners of 2009.

There are also parallels here with the exponential growth model I talked about earlier. With a robust asymmetrical trading strategy, it's always best to cut your losses early but let profits run. It can be tempting to sell a trade quickly if it seems to be going your way. With a clearly defined end goal, however, it's best to hang on if you believe the investment will reach that amount.

Overall, asymmetric trading is a good way to maximise returns in your corporate investment strategy by focussing on returns where the upside outweighs the downside. The most impactful way to use it is to integrate it into your diversified portfolio to build your overall returns while still maintaining some safer, less volatile assets. Even a modest allocation to this type of high-growth investment can make a significant improvement over time.

Afterword

It is right and proper that any entrepreneur should think long and hard about what they want to achieve and what success looks like to them. It is also understandable if, after reading this, you still have some residual doubts about the strategy. *I'm not an investor*, you might be thinking, *I don't know anything about the markets, bonds or FX*. That may well be and there is no shame in thinking in this way, but turn those thoughts on their head and think about how you tackled starting your business in the first place. Like everyone with entrepreneurial instincts, you'll be skilled and knowledgeable about some subjects but a bit ropey on others. Where possible, you'll have brought in expertise from someone who specialises in the areas where you are weak. When money is tight, you've most likely buckled down and worked out what needed to be done by yourself.

When it comes to investing, I would always advise seeking expert advice. Whatever our knowledge of our own sectors, we can't conquer everything alone. Regardless of who we are, what we know and what we have achieved, we all still have much to learn elsewhere. Plus, at the risk of stating the obvious, the profits in your business are the most valuable commodity you own; therefore, it makes sense to make them work as hard as they possibly can. As outlined here, this strategy is not risky as long as you are measured and analytical. A qualified advisor will, however, bring insight, expertise and invaluable experience which will help you to make the best choices. The results will be even stronger, so bringing in trained and skilled outsiders will pay for itself.

When it comes to the best way to find the right investment partner, there are lots of resources online, with multiple organisations set up to advise on corporate investing. As always, a recommendation is always the strongest option. If you don't know anyone who has gone down this path, I would advise doing your due diligence, just as you would with any supplier. Then, once you appoint an advisor, be prepared to listen to their advice and learn from their expertise. While you should always value their opinion, don't be afraid to question any recommendations and offer some alternative suggestions of your own. Even though this might be unfamiliar ground at the moment, you will likely have some sound ideas on what investments will add value and enhance your portfolio. A little bit of market knowledge can go a long way too. It won't be wasted time to do some of your own research about what is happening in the world. Understand what is influencing the markets, which companies, sectors or economies are strong or weak and why things are changing. Don't underestimate the power of networking either. It works for us in a business context and you can rest assured it works in an investment one too. Often a small snippet of information is all you need to spark an idea about a possibly lucrative investment stream.

It is worth reminding yourself that the 'you' as an investor is still the same 'you' as a business owner. The qualities I most admire in any business leader are their instinctive understanding of what will work, why a certain approach will be needed and how it can happen. When you bring these qualities to your investment strategy, together with your passion, innovation, resilience, attention to detail and even creativity, you will reap the benefits. This strategy is not a side hustle. It is a crucial part of your long-term business plan. What you achieve here will impact on every other aspect of your day-to-day operations.

Yes, you will need to make some adjustments to your working day as you become an investor as well as an entrepreneur. Even if you work with an advisor, you will still need to make decisions about what investments suit your business and its current stage of growth. If you were previously focussed on the exit, you will need to change your expectations and forget about collecting that final trophy, but that is not a bad thing – far from it. You can still maintain the vision for your business, and all the obsessive passion that goes with it, but you can now funnel it in a way that will be ultimately more productive. (If you are worried you won't ever have that big celebration that goes with the exit, don't be. By the time most people get to that stage, *if* they reach that stage, they are often too exhausted and punch-drunk to mark the big occasion. It is far better to enjoy the journey.) There is no secret trick I can offer you to help you change your mindset away from all things exit. Once you commit to this strategy and start to see the results, however, you will come to appreciate that you are already achieving your full potential.

To start with, it may feel unfamiliar and like there is a lot to understand and learn. If you begin to feel at all lost, or are unsure of what to do, think about how you would react if you were in the same position when running your day-to-day business. You would tackle the problem analytically, being clear about your vision, the resources you have, or need, to fulfil it and the steps you need to take. The planning stage outlined in chapter three is a crucial part of this strategy. I would suggest that you review your plans regularly, at least every week, so you always know where you are and where you need to be. Things will change, however carefully you set out your stall, and you always need to be on top of that with the same insight, control and clarity you had when you first set out your plan. This intense process will also help you spot opportunities well before anyone else, which is the key to good investing.

Just as in business, there will be ups and downs with your investments, good days and bad days. You may even make some mistakes. If you have a plan and follow the strategies outlined here, however, such as reinvesting for exponential growth and asymmetrical investing, the good days will easily outweigh the bad ones. This is all that is needed for a successful investment programme. Keep a cool head, stick with the plan and you will see results. The value you are adding to your business will increase week by week, month by month and year by year. Forget all about the big single transaction. This is *the* most effective way to receive recognition and reward for your success in business.

Notes

1. To be defined as a micro-entity, a company must meet two of the following criteria:
   - Turnover of £632,000 or less
   - Balance sheet asset of up to £316,000
   - Average of ten employees or fewer
2. 'The realities about selling businesses that they don't tell you', UK Business Brokers (no date), https://ukbusinessbrokers.com/harsh-realities-of-selling-a-small-business, accessed 31 December 2024
3. M Teo, '8 jobs that will disappear by 2030', Power to Fly (no date), https://powertofly.com/up/8-jobs-that-will-disappear, accessed 31 December 2024
4. P Wormley, 'Business succession planning in the era of baby boomer retirement', Hadley (5 February 2021), www.hadleycapital.com/insights/managing-a-small-business/business-succession-planning, accessed 31 December 2024
5. G Gouraige, 'OK, boomer', NewEdge Wealth (7 February 2024), www.newedgewealth.com/ok-boomer/, accessed 31 December 2024
6. C Diiorio, '10,000 boomers are retiring daily – how this changes banking and your finances', Yahoo Finance (2 June 2024), https://finance.yahoo.com/news/10-000-boomers-retiring-daily-160054105.html, accessed 31 December 2024
7. 'Voices of our ageing population: living longer lives', Office for National Statistics (2 November 2022), www.ons.gov.uk/peoplepopulationandcommunity/birthsdeathsandmarriages/ageing/articles

/voicesofourageingpopulation/livinglongerlives, accessed 31 December 2024

8. G Marks, 'Boomers are selling businesses to millennials in a generational handover', The Guardian (18 August 2024), www.theguardian.com/business/article/2024/aug/18/small-business-boomer-millennial-wealth, accessed 31 December 2024

9. A Schroeder, *The Snowball: Warren Buffett and the Business of Life* (Bloomsbury Publishing, 16 September 2009)

10. London Stock Exchange: www.londonstockexchange.com

11. G Wearden, 'FTSE 100 ends year up 3.8% but trails rival markets in Europe and US', The Guardian (29 December 2023), www.theguardian.com/business/2023/dec/29/ftse-100-up-but-europe-us-uk-wall-street-sp-500, accessed 31 December 2024

12. Kalinda, 'A deeper understanding of how compounding works', Endeavour Wealth Management (2023), www.endeavourwealth.ca/post/a-deeper-understanding-of-how-compounding-works, accessed 31 December 2024

13. Moneyfacts: https://moneyfactscompare.co.uk/

14. 'Consumer price inflation, UK: August 2024', Office for National Statistics (18 September 2024), www.ons.gov.uk/economy/inflationandpriceindices/bulletins/consumerpriceinflation/august2024, accessed 31 December 2024

15. GuruFocus, 'Warren Buffett: Investing in Turnarounds Is Difficult', Yahoo! Finance (7 November 2019), https://finance.yahoo.com/news/warren-buffett-investing-turnarounds-difficult-212228594.html, accessed 26 February 2025

16. C Archer, 'What are the average returns of the FTSE 100?', IG (last updated: 23 December 2024), www.ig.com/uk/trading-strategies/what-are-the-average-returns-of-the-ftse-100--230511, accessed 31 December 2024

17. Hargreaves Lansdown: www.hl.co.uk

18. 'UK house price index summary: January 2024', GOV.UK (20 March 2024), www.gov.uk/government/statistics/uk-house-price-index-for-january-2024/uk-house-price-index-summary-january-2024, accessed 31 December 2024

19. S Walmsley, 'General Election 2024: Labour plans to end section 21 must work for renters and responsible landlords', NRLA (13 June 2024), www.nrla.org.uk/news/labour-plans-to-end-section-21-must-work

-for-renters-and-responsible-landlords-copy, accessed
26 February 2025

20. E Yip, 'Startup fail, scale and exit rates in the UK', Beauhurst
(15 September 2022), www.beauhurst.com/blog/startup
-fail-scale-exit, accessed 31 December 2024

21. E Yip, 'Startup fail, scale and exit rates in the UK', Beauhurst
(15 September 2022), www.beauhurst.com/blog/startup
-fail-scale-exit, accessed 31 December 2024

22. A Killian, 'What is forex and how does it work?', IG (no
date), www.ig.com/uk/forex/what-is-forex-and-how
-does-it-work, accessed 31 December 2024

23. 'How much is the minimum Forex trading profit per day?',
Carlos & Company (no date), https://carlosandcompany
.com/forex-trading-profit-per-day, accessed
31 December 2024

24. K Jansen, 'Tony Robbins: how to invest like a
multibillionaire', Nasdaq (26 April 2024), www
.nasdaq.com/articles/tony-robbins:-how-to-invest-like
-a-multibillionaire, accessed 31 December 2024

25. 'The views of Paul Tudor Jones on the trend following
system', Trend Following (no date), www.trendfollowing
.com/paul-tudor-jones, accessed 31 December 2024

The Author

Phil Taylor-Guck is a serial entrepreneur and investor in business, he is currently developing challenger brands, running a marketplace for alternative assets, and heading a global financial services and commodities trading group. Phil is the author of the acclaimed *Gold Rush 2020*, *The Last Dollar*, *The Great Stagflation* and *Alternative Investments*, all published by Rethink Press.

You can connect with Phil Taylor-Guck via:

🌐 https://electholdings.com

www.ingramcontent.com/pod-product-compliance
Lightning Source LLC
Chambersburg PA
CBHW011933190326
41519CB00029B/7508